A COMPLETE BOOK OF

REIKI HEALING

BRIGITTE MÜLLER • HORST H.GÜNTHER

A COMPLETE BOOK

OF

REIKI HEALING

HEAL YOURSELF, OTHERS, AND THE WORLD AROUND YOU

LIFERHYTHM

Translated from the German by Teja Gerken.
Edited by Dixie Black Shipp.
Photographs by Nick Durrer, Switzerland and Horst H. Günther, Germany.
Illustrations by Atelier Deuschl, Germany.
Cover painting by Sharon Maia Nichols.

Library of Congress Cataloging-in-Publication Data
Müller, Brigitte
    [Reiki. English]
    A complete book of Reiki healing: heal yourself, others, and the world
    around you / Brigitte Müller, Horst H. Günther ; [translated
    from the German by Teja Gerken].
    Includes bibliographical references.
    ISBN 0-949795-16-7 $15.95
    1. Reiki (Healing system) I. Günther, Horst H.
    II Title
    RZ403.R45M8513

Copyright © LifeRhythm 1995
    PO Box 806
    Mendocino CA 95460
    Telephone: (707) 937-1825 Fax (707) 937-3052
    Printed in the United States of America.

TABLE OF CONTENTS

Publisher's Note

The treatments and results explained in this book are based on decades of experience. The healing power of Reiki has helped the authors as well as countless others. However, the authors and the publisher of this book remind you that a medical doctor may need to be consulted before treating an illness. Although Reiki flows freely, be aware that you carry the responsibility for how, when and to whom you apply Reiki.

THANKS

Our gratitude goes to the divine power of the universe, which enables us to transmit the gift of healing hands to this planet through Reiki initiations. We also thank the following individuals:

Dr. Mikao Usui, who after searching for many years, rediscovered Reiki;

Dr. Chujiro Hayashi and Mrs. Hawayo Takata;

and especially to Phyllis Lei Furumoto, who initiated both of us as Reiki masters.

We would also like to thank our parents and everyone who has supported us and Reiki in the past years through words and action;

our universal gratitude extends to all our teachers, as well as to our students, who have also been teachers;

and all our Reiki friends who have shared their experiences with us.

DEDICATION

In love and gratitude, we dedicate this book to:

Dr. Mikao Usui

Dr. Chujiro Hayashi

Hawayo Takata

Phyllis Lei Furumoto

to the healing and harmony of this planet with all its forms of life,
to all those who are searching,
and all those who have received the gift of Reiki.

1

WHAT IS REIKI?

Reiki is an ancient healing art, which channels universal life energy through the hands of a practitioner into the body of a receiver. Because it is a universal, God-given power, Reiki belongs to anyone who is ready to receive the gift of healing hands. Anyone, even children, can easily learn it, no special knowledge is needed except the initiation and transmission of power through a Reiki Master.

Reiki is a Japanese word meaning universal life energy. The universe—the space around us–is filled with endless and inexhaustible energy. It is this universal, pristine, and productive source of power and energy that also keeps us alive. Reiki is this natural healing energy, and it flows through the hands of the Reiki channel in a powerful and concentrated form.

We are all born with this universal life energy, but as we go through life we become less open and the flow becomes less pure and free.

Rei	means universal life energy
Ki	is a part of *Rei* and it flows through every–thing alive, including our own individual vital life energy.
Ki	is known to Christians as *light*, to the Chinese as *Chi*, to Hindus as *Prana*, and to Kahunas as *Mana*. It is also called *Bioplasma* or *Cosmic Energy*.

Reiki was rediscovered in Japan in the 19th century by a Christian monk named Dr. Mikao Usui, who found references to it in a 2500 year old Sanskrit document written by one of Buddha's disciples. In the Usui System of Reiki, the healing energy is spontaneously and effortlessly transmitted from one's own body to another organism, through the touch of hands. The strength of the energy depends on the need of the receiver. Reiki goes through any kind of material such as clothing, plaster, bandages, metal, etc. The healer, being a channel, only transmits the universal life energy, no personal energy is taken from the healer; on the contrary, both giver and receiver are simultaneously strengthened and enriched with energy.

In giving Reiki, we are more than just a channel; we *become* Reiki, and we *are* universal life energy. It is the God within us who accomplishes this powerful task. It is not our ego, it is the *I am* presence, the divine self in us through which the healing takes place. Self healing energies are awakened through the transmission of Reiki, because one can only heal oneself. Because of this, both the Reiki practitioner, as well as the person receiving Reiki are experiencing *self healing* during the treatment. Anyone seeking or wanting to give healing can become a Reiki channel. Reiki does not conflict with any religious or meditative practices or rituals; it will only enrich and strengthen their universality.

Reiki supports medical treatments such as massages, foot reflexology, cosmetic massages, acupressure, acupuncture, chiropractic treatments, breath therapy, lymph drainages, psychotherapy etc. It is effective wherever hands touch, because Reiki hands radiate healing energy at any time in any place. Because of this, Reiki is especially helpful to those in healing professions.

Reiki brings the body and mind into an even balance and works on all levels: the physical, spiritual, emotional and soul level. Reiki encourages self–healing, strengthens body and soul, opens blocks, balances the chakras, rebuilds harmony and flows in unlimited quantity. Through Reiki you will experience the blessing of spiritual growth and change. Reiki is the divine grace of God, an immeasurable gift.

2

The History of Reiki's Usui System

Until this century, the history of Reiki was transmitted from teacher to student mainly through an oral tradition.

Dr. Mikao Usui, the founder of Reiki, lived in Kyoto, Japan toward the end of the 19th century and served as a Christian priest and leader of a small local university. At one of his Sunday services, he was asked by one of his students if he took the word of the Bible literally. Usui affirmed that he did, but his student still was not satisfied with the answer. He asked: "In the Bible it says that Jesus made the sick healthy, that he cured them, that he walked on water. Do you believe that Jesus walked on water, simply because it is written? Have you ever experienced something like this yourself?" "No," said Usui, "I have never experienced such a thing. But I do have faith in the words of the Bible." The student replied: "Maybe this blind faith is enough for you, but I would like to see these things with my own eyes."

This dialogue brought great change to Usui's life. The next day he quit his work and traveled to the United States to attend the University of Chicago. There he studied ancient Christian writings and received a doctorate in Ancient Languages. He was always trying to understand the secret of the healings by Jesus Christ and his disciples, but he was unable to find what he was looking for.

During his studies he had learned that Buddha also had the power to heal. He decided to return to Japan in search of further Buddhist teachings. Back in his homeland, he traveled to many monasteries. This is how he finally met an older Abbot in a Zen monastery who was also interested in healing. He stayed in the monastery and began to search the old Buddhist writings—the Sutras—for the key to healing. At first he studied the Japanese translations

Dr. Mikao Usui

of the Sutras. Because he could not find an answer, he learned Chinese. But even in the Chinese translations of the Sutras he could not find any leads.

Usui did not give up. He learned Sanskrit so that he could read the original Buddhist writings. Finally, in an ancient Sanskrit document, written by an unknown disciple of Buddha's, he found what he had been searching for for seven years. It was the symbology and description of how Buddha healed.

He had thus rediscovered the knowledge but he still lacked the power to heal. Following a consultation with the Abbot, he decided to go to a holy mountain in Japan to fast and meditate for 21 days. He placed 21 small rocks on the ground in front of him to serve as a calendar, removing one every day. During these days, he read the Sutras, sang and meditated.

It was still very dark, in the middle of the 21st day, when Dr. Usui finished his meditation and prayed fervently, "Father, please show me the light!" Suddenly, rapidly moving toward him in the sky, he saw a bright light. It became bigger and bigger as it came toward him, and hit the middle of his forehead, at the third eye. He fell to the ground, lost his sense of consciousness and moved into a trance–like state of being. In this higher state of consciousness he saw many rainbow colored bubbles; blue, turquoise, lavender and pink. The symbols he had earlier seen in the Sanskrit–Sutra appeared in front of him in golden letters as if they were on a giant screen.

This was the key to the healing powers of Buddha and Jesus. This enlightening experience marks the beginning of the Usui System of Reiki.

The sun was high in the sky when Usui regained consciousness. To his surprise, he was full of energy, and not exhausted or hungry like the day before. Usui hurried on his way back to the monastry and stumbled, injuring his big toe. He held his hand over it, and the bleeding stopped; the pain went away.

Soon he found a hostel where he ordered a meal. While he waited, the keeper's daughter came in with a painful face and a swollen red cheek. She had a toothache. Usui asked her for permission to touch her face. He held both cheeks in his hands, and within minutes the swelling went down and the pain went away. "You are no ordinary monk," said the very surprised girl.

Upon his return to the monastery, he learned that the Abbot was in bed with arthritis. After he rested, Usui applied his healing hands; the Abbot's pain eased.

Dr. Chujiro Hayashi

After a few weeks in the monastery, Usui decided to go into the slums of Kyoto to heal the sick there. He healed many and sent everyone who was young and able out to look for work. After seven years had passed, he realized he was seeing the same familiar faces again and again, returning to the slums in the same condition in which he had first found them.

He was very discouraged, and asked them why they had come back. They told him they preferred to live as they had previously lived, and did not show any gratitude towards life.

Usui was shattered, and realized that although he had healed their bodies from the symptoms of illness, he had not taught them a new way of life. This caused him to create the *Reiki Rules of Life*. (Hawayo Takata passed these on in her journal):

> *Just for today —Thou shalt not anger*
> *Just for today—Thou shalt not worry*
> *Be thankful for the many blessings.*
> *Earn thy living with honest labor*
> *Be kind to thy neighbors.*

Given our many experiences and recent realizations about positive thinking, the authors have adapted these Rules of Life for today's age, and brought them into a more contemporary form.

Dr. Hawayo Takata

SPIRITUAL RULES OF LIFE:

Just for today
be free and happy.
Just for today
have joy.
Just for today you are taken care of.
Live consciously in the moment.
Count your blessings with gratitude.
Honor your parents, teachers and elders.
Earn your living honestly.
Love your neighbor as you love yourself.
Show gratitude to all living things.

Usui left the slums of Kyoto and began to teach. He taught people to heal themselves and he passed his rules of life on so that people could heal their minds as well as their bodies.

Dr. Chujiro Hayashi, a retired Marine's Officer, wanted to serve humankind, and became Usui's student. He was initiated by Usui and felt a deep vocation to practice Reiki. Hayashi became Usui's closest assistant, and as Usui got closer to the end of his life he made Hayashi a Reiki Master and trusted him to keep and care for all the teachings.

Hayashi founded the Reiki Healing Clinic in Tokyo. There, Reiki was taught and used to treat patients. From Hayashi's documents it is clear that he believed that Reiki finds the cause of physical symptoms, which it then balances with the right vibrations (or fills with energy), so that health is reestablished.

Hawayo Takata, a young woman from Hawaii, came to Japan in 1935 to have a tumor surgically removed. During the preparations for the operation she heard an inner voice telling her that the operation was not necessary and that there was another way for her to be healed. After she talked with the doctor, she was taken to the Hayashi Clinic by his nurse, Ms. Shimura. She stayed in the Reiki clinic for several months, receiving daily Reiki treatments.

Phyllis Lei Furumoto

As her health returned, she wanted to learn Reiki herself. At first she was not accepted as a student, and she realized that she had to show a deep inner commitment towards Reiki. She went to Hayashi and told him about her feelings and her preparedness to stay in Japan as long as necessary. Dr. Hayashi agreed, and her training began.

Hawayo Takata and her two daughters stayed with the Hayashi family for one year. She gave daily Reiki treatments and continued to study and learn. When her training was finished she returned to Hawaii with the gift of healing hands.

She was a successful healer in Hawaii. In 1938 she was visited by Hayashi and his daughter. She received further training, and in February of 1938 was initiated by Dr. Hayashi to be a Master of the Usui System of natural healing. Soon afterwards Hayashi and his daughter traveled back to Japan.

In 1941, Hayashi anticipated there would be a war between the United States and Japan, but could not reconcile his work as a Reiki Master with his expected service in the Japanese Marines.

At this time, Hawayo Takata had a dream which prompted her to visit Hayashi in Japan. They talked about the war they expected, and about where she should go to protect herself and the teachings of Reiki.

When everything was discussed between them and they had agreed on a way to proceed, Hayashi named Hawayo Takata as his successor. He said his goodbyes to everyone and then, dressed in customary Japanese tradition, sat in the lotus position, closed his eyes and left his body.

Takata returned to Hawaii a Reiki Master. She became known as a powerful healer and teacher, who introduced the gift of Reiki to the western world. As far as it is known, she was the only living Reiki Master until 1976. At that time she began to train and initiate some of her students to be Reiki Masters. Until her death in 1980 she initiated twenty-one Reiki Masters, including her granddaughter Phyllis Lei Furumoto.

Phyllis had received the 1st grade Reiki Initiation as a child. Later in the 1970's she received the 2nd grade initiation. In the spring of 1979 Phyllis was initiated as a Reiki Master and began to travel with her grandmother. What followed were intensive lessons and training as Phyllis learned from her grandmother that she was to become her successor. Shortly before Takata's death in December of 1980, she received the trust to continue the spiritual Reiki line as its Grand Master.

In the spring of 1982 a group of Reiki Masters gathered with Phyllis Lei Furumoto in Hawaii to honor the memory of Hawayo Takata and they agreed to meet yearly. At the second meeting "The Reiki Alliance" was founded. The main objective of the conference was to acknowledge Phyllis Lei Furumoto as the grand master in direct spiritual descent from Mikao Usui, Chujiro Hayashi and Hawayo Takata.

We, the authors, were also initiated by Phyllis Lei Furumoto: Brigitte Müller in 1983 in Canada, and Horst Günther in July of 1985 in the United States. It means very much to us to keep to the tradition of Usui's teachings and to pass it on.

In the spring of 1988 Phyllis Lei Furumoto gave her blessing and empowerment to those Reiki Masters who felt ready and were able to train and initiate new Reiki Masters. The Masters who take on this enormous responsibility need to have several years of Reiki workshop experience,and must have the requisite knowledge, skill and energy, as they carry the initiating Masters' energy.

In the last few years, Reiki has spread unusually fast around the world. This will contribute to the fulfillment of the world's desire for healing, harmony, love and brotherhood, and will ultimately bring peace to the whole planet.

3

In Memory of
Mrs. Hawayo Takata

We know that Hawayo Takata played a powerful role in the transmission of Reiki. Because she grew up in Hawaii, Reiki was not lost to the Western Hemisphere as a secret Japanese art, or lost altogether through the second world war. We remember and honor her with special gratitude.

The following is an excerpt from an interview with Hawayo Takata printed in *The Times,* of San Mateo, May 17, 1975:

> Reiki? What is Reiki? Mrs. Hawayo (which means Hawaii) Takata, 74, of Hawaii, the Master of Reiki explains: "Reiki means Universal Life Energy." It is not a religion. "It was explained to me this way: 'Here is the great space which surrounds us—the Universe. There is endless and enormous energy in it. It is universal...its ultimate source is the Creator...It is a limitless force. It is the source of energy that makes the plants grow...the birds fly.'
>
> Mrs. Takata adds in her words, "It is Nature. It is God, the power He makes available to His children who seek it. In Japanese this is *Reiki*."
>
> Skeptics may quit now. It is interesting to note, however that Mrs. Takata points out that the American Medical Association of Hawaii permits Reiki treatments in hospitals, whenever requested by a patient. Also, Mrs. Takata will teach Reiki at the University of Hawaii this winter, for which she has a signed contract. She is living proof that something is very right. At age 74 she plays nine holes of golf daily when at at home and participates in 18-hole golf tournaments. She is tiny—and mighty, projecting tranquility, quiet strength and power.
>
> She was not always so. Mrs. Takata recalls when she was 29 her husband died and she was left penniless with two small daughters. "By the time I was 35 I had all kinds of ailments, appendicitis, a benign

tumor, gallstones and to top it, I had asthma, so could not undergo an operation requiring anesthetic. I lost so much weight. Over a period of seven years I was further emotionally devastated; one dear member of my family died each year. I was a church-going woman and had always believed in God. One day I meditated and finally said 'God, I am up against the wall...Help me.' I said to myself, 'If God hears, He will help...'As far as I am concerned, that is what happened. I heard a voice. Today we call that clairaudience. I didn't know anything about that in 1935. I heard a voice speak after I complained so bitterly. I felt all alone in the world, as if I alone had all the suffering, burdens, poverty. I had said 'Why am I poor? Why do I have such illness and pain? Why do I have all the sorrows?' The voice which replied was loud and clear; it spoke three times. It said 'No—Get rid of all your illness. Just like that you will find health, happiness and security.'

"I couldn't believe my ears until I heard the same message three times. Within 21 days I was on a boat to Tokyo, hoping to find help there. I went to the Maeda Orthopedic Hospital in the district of Akasaka in Tokyo. That is the finest district in the heart of Tokyo near the Royal Palace. The hospital was named after my friend, Dr. T. Maeda, whom I went to see."

Mrs. Takata says that when Dr. Maeda saw her, she was gone down to 97 pounds. He shook his head and said she would have to build up her strength before any thought of surgery. She and her two small daughters stayed at the hospital. After 21 days in the hospital, Mrs. Takata was ready for surgery and was on the operating table being prepared when suddenly again heard the commanding voice. This time it said "Do not have the operation. It is not necessary." Mrs. Takata said she pinched herself to make sure she was both conscious and sane. Three times she heard the admonition and suddenly got off the operating table and stood on the floor causing great consternation among the nurses. Dr. Maeda came in and she told him she was not afraid of dying but wanted to know if there was any other form of treatment. The doctor asked how long she would stay in Japan and when she told him two years, he told the nurse to dress her and called his sister, Mrs. Shimura, then the hospital dietician.

Mrs. Takata later learned Mrs. Shimura had nearly died of dysentery years before and was in a coma when she was taken to the Reiki Master,

Dr. Chijuro Hayashi. She had a miraculous recovery. Now Mrs. Shimura took Mrs. Takata to Dr. Hayashi's offices. "Two of his practitioners worked on me" she recalls. "One on the head, sinus, the thyroid, thymus, glands; the other on the rest of the body. I can best describe it as it is referred to in the Bible, the 'laying on of hands.' The Maeda Hospital had not yet forwarded my medical history, yet they they diagnosed my illness perfectly. On my third treatment, my curiosity became boundless. I didn't know what to think. I was obviously improving. I was still staying at the Maeda Hospital where they checked and confirmed my progress.

"I am a very curious woman. I said to myself, 'I am going to investigate how they are doing this. What makes me feel first the warmth then actual heat emanating from these hands? I looked under the table, at the ceiling, everywhere. I could find no cords or instruments. Then I thought, 'Aha, they have a battery hidden in their sleeves.' Dr. Hayashi's assistants wore the Japanese kimono with long sleeves which hold pockets. They worked so silently. There was no talking. My moment came. When I was being treated, I suddenly grabbed the practitioner by the pocket. He was startled, but thinking I needed some tissue, he thoughtfully handed me some. I said, 'No, I want to see the machine in your pocket.' He burst into loud laughter. Dr. Hayashi came in to see what the commotion was all about. " He smiled and shook his head Mrs. Takata recalls. He proceeded to give her the explanation of a Universal Life Force. He said, "Whenever you feel the contact, all I know is that I have reached this great Universal Life Force and it comes through me to you—these are the electrodes," and he held up his hands. "That force begins to revitalize and restore the balance of your entire system."

In time Mrs. Takats became convinced she too, should learn more and become a student of Dr. Hayashi. She adds, "I passed my examinations perfectly."

"I speak with confidence about this" Mrs. Takata notes, "but please understand I do not speak as 'I'—I speak because it is God's power. He is the One who makes it available to us. " Mrs. Takata is the only teacher of the Usui system of Reiki in the world today and she is recognized as its Master.

Hawayo Takata's Recipes

Mrs. Takata had her own health recipes. The following are two of her recommendations:

Garden Salad

> 1 small cabbage, finely cut
> 2–3 medium size red beets, grated raw
> 4 celery sticks, finely cut
> 1 small head of cauliflower, finely cut
> 1 apple (can be added for a special taste variation)

> This would make a very large serving. It is recommended to reduce the size of the ingredients to make a fresh salad every day.

Takata's Rejuvenating Drink

> 1 grapefruit
> 3 small red beets, peeled
> 2 handfuls of cut cabbage
> 1 1/2 cups of water
> 4 tablespoons peeled almonds
> 4 tablespoons sunflower seeds

> Mix in blender until completely liquid, then add 6 tablespoons Lecithin powder and 2 tablespoons brewers yeast. Now take half of this mixture and add a half gallon of spring water. Drink several glasses daily.

4

How to Become a Reiki Channel

One does not need any previous experience to become a Reiki practitioner, but the healing power of Reiki can, in general, only be *transmitted* through a Reiki Master. A person should have an open heart, the desire to receive the Reiki transmission and carry the intention to use it. If one wants to heal themselves and their family, other people, animals or plants, then the channel will open for the healing energy during the Reiki instruction.

Preparation and Initiation for the 1st Grade

The 1st Grade is given during a weekend or on four consecutive days or evenings, in sessions lasting three to four hours each. Sometimes it will also be given during a holiday workshop. During the workshop, the Reiki Master undertakes four initiations or "power transmissions." These will prepare the students and open their inner healing channels. Each initiation is a blessing and healing. What happens is a kind of a cleansing on all levels, affecting the body, mind and soul, and raising the vibrational frequency of all participants. Blocks and toxins are released, and healing is encouraged. The transmission of energy may also cause self–healing reactions which will mostly cease after the workshop.

You will receive the basic training and hand positions to give yourself Reiki. Often participants feel the flow of Reiki after the first initiation and learn to exchange the universal life energy with other members of the workshop. Reiki flows depending on the need of the receiver, who only takes as much as is needed. You feel clearly that you only act as a channel and that none of your own energy is taken. On the contrary, you are being charged simultaneously and self healing is taking place. The flow of this loving, healing, soft and powerful energy is an uplifting experience.

Reiki will change your life, and accelerate your mental and physical healing as well as your spiritual growth, so you will clearly feel the connection with your inner self and will be touched with your own love. Because of this, harmony and peace flows with yourself and your world again. Reiki also helps you to have the courage to change those things in your life that you want to change. By the end of the workshop you have received the gift of healing hands. Every person heals themselves! Now you have the tools to do so. Take responsibility in yourself, change your thoughts and behavior according to the "Spiritual Rules of Life," and you will become a new human being with much more joy in life.

PREPARATION AND INITIATION FOR THE 2ND GRADE.

Traditionally, the Usui System of Reiki is taught in two grades. When you have completed the 1st grade and have used Reiki actively in your life, then you can deepen your connection with Reiki and your own spiritual growth through the initiation into the 2nd grade. At least three months should pass between the initiations of the 1st and the 2nd grade. Only in exceptional cases can one receive the 2nd grade earlier. You should feel within yourself when the time is right to receive the 2nd grade, as there will be much movement on many levels. Be ready for further change in your life.

The 2nd grade is called *Oku Den,* or "deep knowledge," and is a psychic opening. It will especially act on the subtle bodies. Your intuition and ability to heal will expand. With your initiation, you receive the secret holy symbols and the specific mantra. These are solely for the use of people initiated into the 2nd grade. Their use carries a large responsibility.

The healing powers multiply through the intiation into the 2nd grade, and you learn to use the symbols to give mental healing and to heal over a distance independently from space and time. Mental healing means that you now possess the ability to connect yourself with the subconsciousness or your higher self, and to initiate healing through the spirit, for example in cases of depression, sleeplessness, nervous breakdowns and addictions. You can also use mental healing on yourself to change rigid patterns of behavior into new, constructive ones.

You become aware that you carry the responsibility for your life and that you are the master of your life and your circumstances. We are all on the way to mastering ourselves, whether it is conscious or not, and we need to learn to use our energies wisely. Everything that we send out comes back to us (the Law of the Circle). If you send out much joy and love, it will return many times over. Thus we must take responsibility for the enhanced energy that we possess after the 2nd grade initiation.

5

Becoming a Reiki Master

In the spring of 1988, Phyllis Lei Furumoto gave her blessing and authorization for the initiation of Masters to all those Reiki Masters who felt willing and able to train and initiate others.

The call to become a Reiki Master is intuitively recognized by those people who have been initiated in the 1st and 2nd grade and who have practiced for some time. The initiation brings with it further personal growth and change on all levels.

We received the blessing and authorization to carry out this training through the initiation and relationship established with Phyllis Lei Furumoto. In great gratitude, we now have brought several Reiki Masters onto this path. We are completely aware of the unending responsibility the Master accepts in initiating a student to the level of a Master.

The program of the training is individually tailored to the personal needs of the person ready for this further step.

6

SUGGESTIONS FOR
REIKI PRACTITIONERS

Reiki flows and works only through the hands of a practitioner who has received the four initiations of the 1st grade, or later the initiations into the 2nd grade through an authorized Reiki Master. Only with this initiation are students enabled to give Reiki to themselves or others. In case you—the reader—have not received a Reiki initiation, we hope that the following descriptions and pictures will be informative and inspiring.

The Reiki practitioner, because of the protection of the initiations, only acts as a channel and simply transmits the universal life energy, so that no personal energy is taken from him. He himself will even be enriched with energy.

For all those who have taken part in a Reiki workshop and are Reiki channels, the following guide to Reiki treatment will serve to deepen their knowledge. It is not important to follow the exact order of the hand positions. One should rather let themselves be guided by Reiki which works by intuition. In our many years of experience in treatment and workshops, the following descriptions have proven to be highly successful. In general one can say, "let Reiki draw your hands to the right position."

7

SELF–HEALING WITH REIKI

After you have received the Reiki initiation of the 1st grade, you should give Reiki to yourself every day to strengthen your health and to charge your "life battery" with energy. This will maintain your physical and mental health, support your spiritual growth and expand your awareness. You become whole, giving yourself love and handling your stress and daily commitments better. In her workshops, Hawayo Takata always recommended beginning with oneself. "You are number one," she said, "and if you still have time afterwards you can give Reiki to your family and friends." We first should love and heal ourselves, because we are only capable of giving to others what we would give ourselves. This is the deeper meaning of saying "love your neighbor as you love yourself."

The more intensively you use Reiki, the stronger the energy grows within you. Simply get used to putting your hands onto your body whenever they are free, for example:

- In the morning after waking up to activate and balance your chakras (this is especially intensive with the use of the symbols of the 2nd grade).

- During the day when making phone calls, in the subway, during rush hour, while watching TV, in the theater, during waiting periods, etc.

- At night in bed to help fall asleep or to sleep through the night.

Reiki can be very helpful in overcoming alcohol or drug addiction, since it reaches deeper levels of awareness. Reiki of the 2nd grade, especially, can reach the subconciousness and transmit the universal life energy onto a new level. It is also recommended that positive affirmations be included in the mental treatment of the 2nd grade.

Give yourself a full Reiki treatment whenever possible. You will become healed and complete in body, mind and spirit.

If a time comes in your life when you don't want to give Reiki to yourself or others, you might have a resistance against your growth and change. In this case it would be good to continue with Reiki as it will open this resistance. Reiki will give you the courage to shape your life the way you like it. All you need to do is give yourself Reiki every day! Reiki is the teacher.

HEAD POSITION SELF–HEALING: H

H 1—Eyes/Sinuses

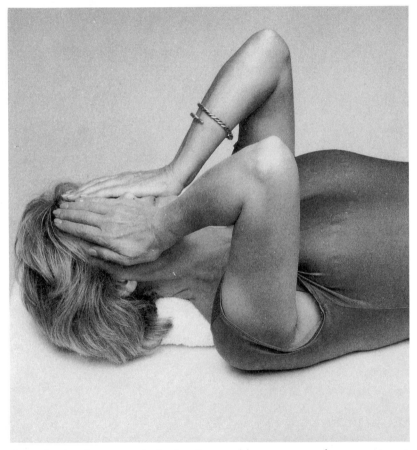

Over forehead, eyes and cheeks. Eye problems, gray and green cataract sinuses • head cold • allergies • asthma • cerebral nerves • pituitary gland • pineal gland. Balances the pituitary and pineal glands. The pineal gland is the central point of hormonal regulation. Very relaxing in stress situations. The 6th chakra (third eye) relates to the 1st chakra.

HEAD POSITION SELF–HEALING: H

H 2A—To the sides of the Head

To the sides of the sinuses, optic nerves. Balances the right brain (intuition, wisdom) and the left brain (rational understanding). Very relaxing in stress situations.

HEAD POSITION SELF–HEALING: H

H 2B—Ears

Over the ears. Many organs can be treated around the ears (acupuncture points: heart, intestines, kidneys, lungs, stomach, liver, gall, etc.). Used for colds and flu, hearing problems, buzzing noises in the ear, loss of balance.

HEAD POSITION SELF–HEALING: H

H 3—Back of the Head

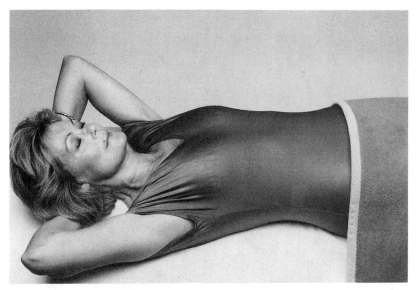

Back of the head, onto Medulla Oblongata. Eyes • vision • headaches • nosebleeds • hay fever sinuses • stroke • digestion • fear • shock • worries. Will calm and clear thoughts. Medulla Oblongata is connected to the third eye.

HEAD POSITION SELF–HEALING: H

H 4—Top of the Head

Across the head. Headaches • eye pains • abdomen cramps • flatulence and digestion problems • bladder • multiple sclerosis • stress and emotions. 7th chakra.

HEAD POSITION SELF–HEALING: H
H 5—Thyroid Gland • Thymus Gland

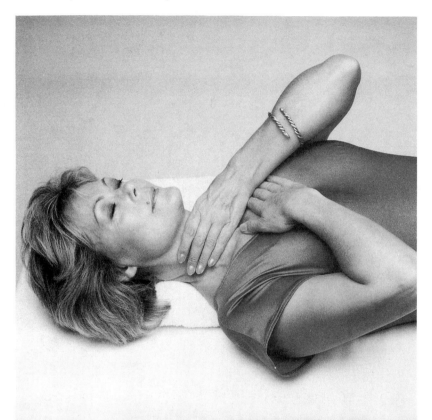

On the sides and the front of the throat. Thyroid gland • important for metabolism • over or underweight • palpitation • angina • flu • high or low blood pressure • anger • frustration • communication • self–expression. 5th chakra, related to the 2nd chakra.

HEAD POSITION SELF-HEALING: H

Special Position—Eyes and Teeth

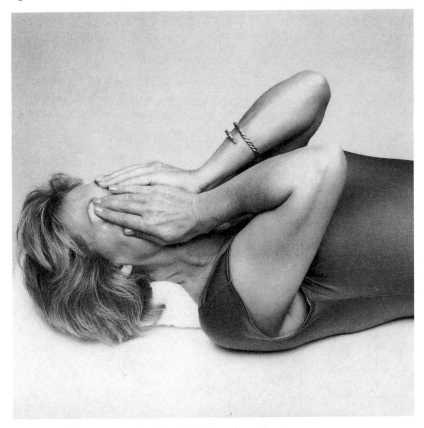

Eyes • teeth • sinuses. For head colds and toothaches.

HEAD POSITION SELF–HEALING: H
Special Position—Eyes

Eyes • sinuses.

HEAD POSITION SELF–HEALING: H

Special Position—To Focus

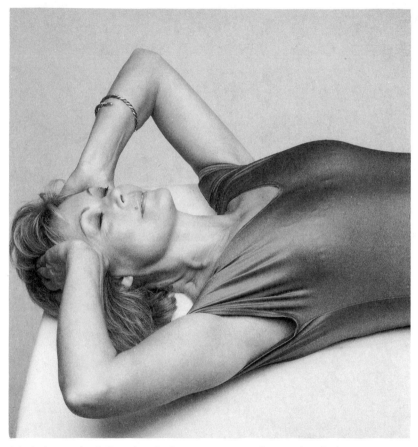

To balance the left and right brain, in cases of stress, headaches.

BASIC POSITION SELF–HEALING (FRONT): BP
BP 1—Right side, Liver/Gall (with G 2 left side)

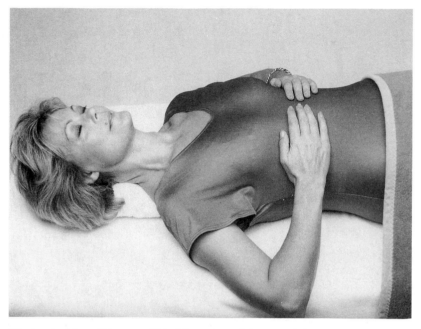

Under the chest. Liver • gallbladder • part of the stomach • pancreas • spleen anemia • leukemia • immune system • infections • Aids • cancer • jaundice • gall–stones • hypoglycemia • diabetes • detoxification • sorrow • anger depression suppressed chronic complaints • loss of balance.

BASIC POSITION SELF–HEALING (FRONT): BP

BP 2—Left side, Pancreas (with G 1 right side)

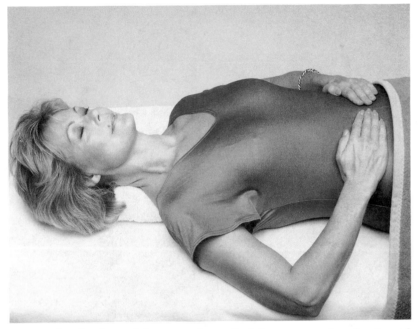

At waist height. Part of the stomach • tail of the pancreas (production of insulin and enzymes) • large intestine • small intestine • anemia • leukemia immune system • diabetes • flu • infections • Aids • cancer.

Basic Position Self–Healing (Front): BP
BP 3—Solar plexus

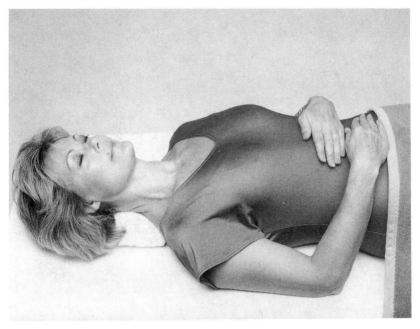

Upper hand on the stomach, lower hand on the navel. Solar plexus • stomach intestines • heart • digestion • lymph • shock • emotions • depression. The Hara is app. 1 inch under the navel, energy center. 3rd chakra.

BASIC POSITION SELF–HEALING (FRONT): BP
BP 4—V–Position Abdomen

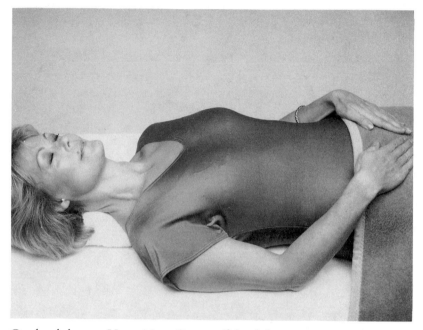

On the abdomen, V–position. Organs of the abdomen • intestines • ovaries • bladder • urethra • cardiovascular • digestion • appendix (right) • breast tumors • cramps • menopause complication • backaches • tumors in the ovaries/uterus/bladder. 1st and 2nd chakra.

Basic Position Self–Healing (Front): BP
BP 5—Heart/Thymus

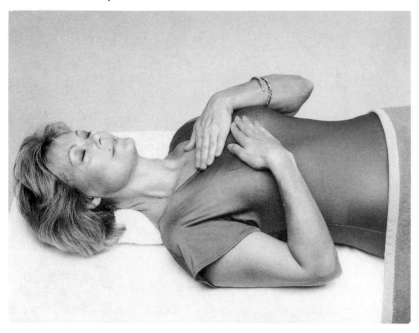

In the Heart Position. Heart • thymus gland • lung • heart ailments • bronchitis • immune system • lymph • deafness • emotions • depressions. 4th chakra.

SPECIAL POSITIONS SELF–HEALING
Special Position—Thighs (inner side)

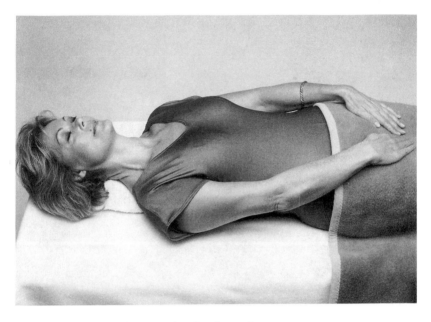

On the inner side of the thigh. Blood circulation.

SPECIAL POSITIONS SELF–HEALING
Special Position—Greater Trochanter—Legs/Gall Bladder

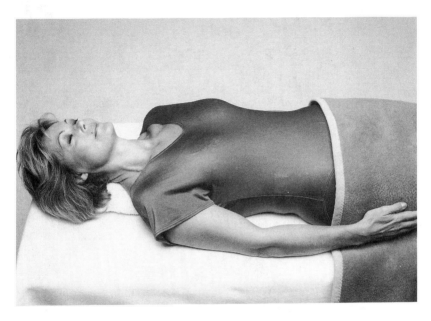

Greater Trochanter. Varicose veins • leg pain • gall point.

SPECIAL POSITIONS SELF–HEALING

Special Position—Breasts

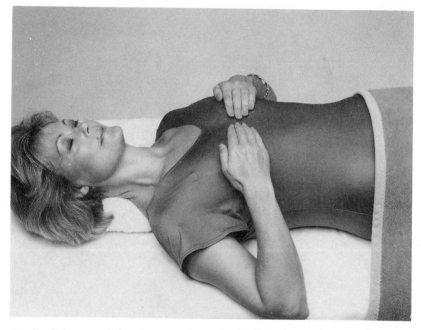

On both breasts. (If not appropriate, give Reiki a few inches away).

BACK POSITION SELF–HEALING: B
B 1—Shoulders/Neck

On the shoulders. Left and right on the shoulders • For stress and tightness.

BACK POSITION SELF–HEALING: B
B 1A—7th Vertebrae (Medulla Oblongata)

In the neck/7th vertebrae (Medulla Oblongata). For pain in the bones, heart
• vertebrae • nerves • shock on the spine • neck problems.

BACK POSITION SELF–HEALING: B

B 3—Kidneys/Adrenal Glands

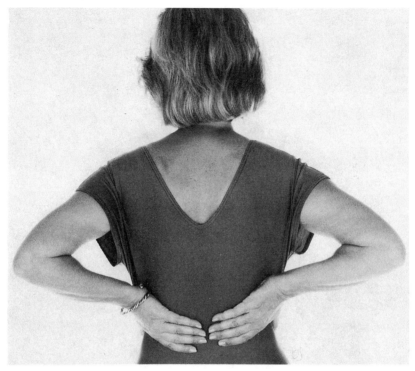

Nerves • heart • lung •adrenal glands • back aches • shock • allergies • hay
fever • stress • detoxification • and as on the front of the body.

BACK POSITION SELF–HEALING: B
B 4—Waist

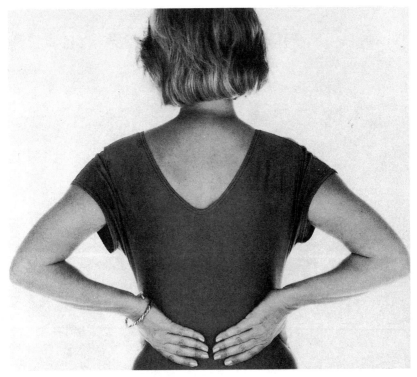

Around the waist. Nerves • lung • kidneys • backaches • shock • allergies • hay fever • stress • detoxification • and as on the front of the body.

BACK POSITION SELF–HEALING: B
B 5—Hip

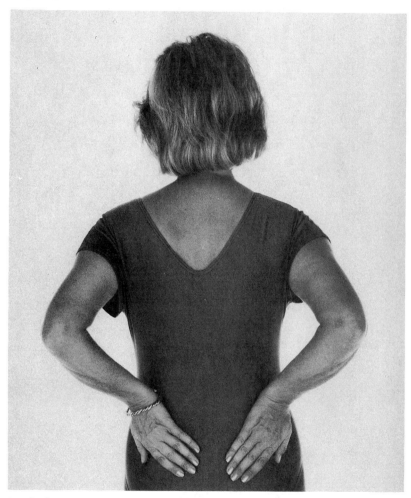

On the hips. Sciatica • lymph • nerves • backaches • hip • and as on the front of the body.

Back Position Self–Healing: B

B 6—Buttocks

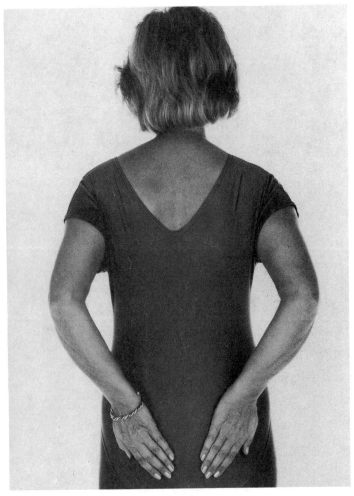

On the buttocks. Sciatica • lymph • nerves • backaches • hips • and as on the front of the body.

8

ANATOMIC ILLUSTRATIONS

In general, it is not necessary to know a great deal about human anatomy or the anatomy of animals in order to give a Reiki treatment. However, it can be very helpful, especially when wanting to treat certain organs more specifically. Following are simple anatomic illustrations of the bodies of humans, dogs, cats and horses. For further studies we recommend an anatomic atlas.

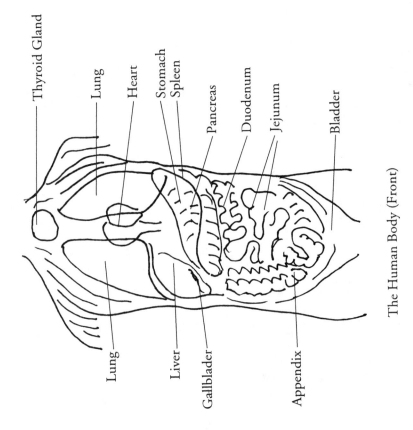

Thyroid Gland

Lung

Heart

Stomach

Spleen

Pancreas

Duodenum

Jejunum

Bladder

Lung

Liver

Gallbladder

Appendix

The Human Body (Front)

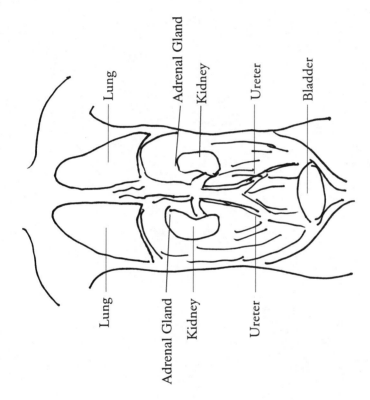

The Human Body (As seen from the back)

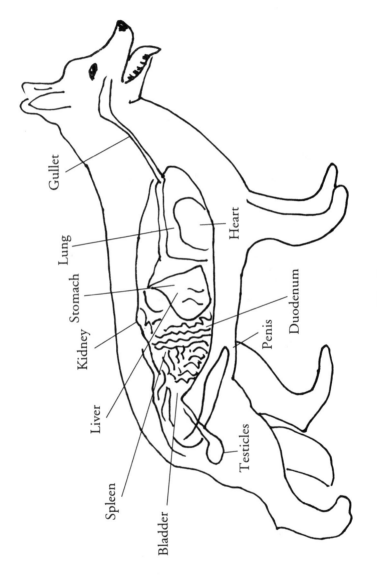

Gullet

Lung

Stomach

Kidney

Liver

Spleen

Bladder

Heart

Duodenum

Penis

Testicles

The Dog

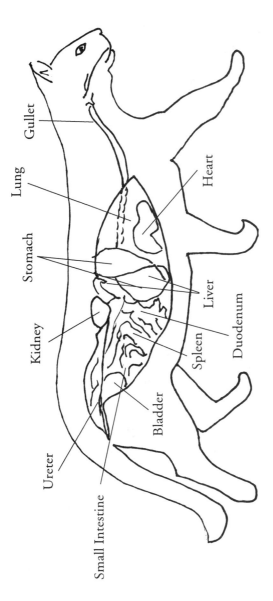

The Cat

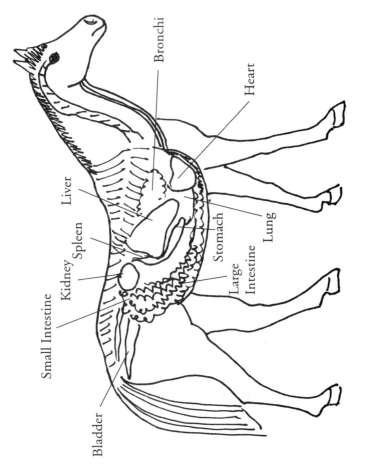

Bronchi

Heart

Liver

Kidney

Spleen

Small Intestine

Bladder

Stomach

Large Intestine

Lung

The Horse

9

Recommendations
for Reiki Treatment

General Recommendations

A complete Reiki treatment is always given except in emergencies and accidents, or when a quick treatment is needed. This is because not only the symptoms, but also the *cause* of an ailment are in need of a treatment in order to bring about a complete healing process. The person giving Reiki is only a channel and thus has no influence on the result of the treatment. This responsibility for healing lies only within the receiving person, and on a deep level which cannot be consciously controlled. When the receiver is ready and open for the healing process, then his self–healing powers are activated through Reiki. The person giving Reiki should be aware that it is not a personal achievement when healing occurs, but the result of a divine force. Hence, one always does "everything right" in giving a Reiki treatment. This is not necessary to analyze, since a reaction in the hands will indicate when the cause of the problem has been found. For example, this could be perceived as a hot or cold feeling. The hands should stay on these places until the energy flow is normalized.

The faith of the person giving Reiki strengthens the healing power. Doubts and unwillingness to receive reduce the ability to have an impact with Reiki. Reiki becomes stronger as it is used, so it is important to use Reiki often. Like an unused muscle, it will atrophy.

Reiki should only be used to help and heal. Reiki will not work if it is used with the wrong intention.

In the beginning of a series of Reiki treatments, the practioner should, if possible, give four treatments on four consecutive days. These four days give the body the opportunity to free itself from its toxins. During this time it is possible to have strong self–healing reactions, so that chronic ailments often appear temporarily. It can also trigger emotional reactions, which are to be judged positively. These kinds of reactions to Reiki healing usually calm down within 12 to 24 hours. After the initial four days, further treatment can be given once or twice a week, or even daily over a period of several weeks, and thus the person's self–healing powers will be brought to a flow.

In general, a Reiki treatment takes about one to one and a half hours, so the practitioner stays in each position for about three to five minutes depending on the energy flow. Specific problem or pain areas can be treated for an extra ten to twenty minutes or even longer. In urgent cases a treatment can last several hours or can be repeated several times a day.

There are exceptions in the duration of a treatment. For example, one could give Reiki to older or very sensitive people for about 30 minutes initially, increasing the time as they get used to it. Twenty to thirty minutes is also enough with small children.

Reiki flows through clothing, plaster, belts and bandages, etc., so that it is not necessary to undress before a treatment.

You should be in a quiet space of mind during the treatment. Create a peaceful atmosphere. Conversations should usually be avoided during treatment, with the exception of psychotherapeutic sessions which are combined with Reiki. Calming, meditative music can be very supporting.

Reiki does not replace a medical doctor's care or medication. However, it supports any kind of therapy and the natural healing processes, as it activates self–healing powers. It is especially helpful before and after surgery; it strengthens, harmonizes and calms the patient. Recovery will be accelerated and the wound will heal faster and better. One can give oneself Reiki with a soothing effect before and after surgery with local anesthesia and at the dentist. One should not give oneself Reiki directly after the anesthesia or during the procedure, our experience shows that this can reduce, delay or prematurely cancel the anesthesia.

Chronic ailments take much longer to improve and they require repeated treatments of several hours, over a longer period of time. In cases of immediate, severe sickness (for example Aids or cancer), Reiki should be given daily for several hours. This means that ideally members of the family should be initiated into Reiki to perhaps give treatments in 24 hour shifts (see also description in the book *Reiki, Hawayo Takata's Story*). In contrast to chronic ailments, one can usually quickly see a positive change in victims of accidents.

If the given circumstances do not allow multiple Reiki treatments, then the rule becomes "a little Reiki is always better than none".

Please remember at the end of a Reiki treatment that you only function as a channel, no matter what happened during the treatment. Be thankful that the healing power was able to flow through you—it is an appropriate time for a prayer of gratitude for grace received.

PRACTICAL DETAILS

- Take off watches and rings.
- Wash your hands with soap before and after the treatment.
- Loosen tight belts, waist bands and neck ties (on the Reiki receiver as well)
- The receiver should take his shoes off and lie relaxed without crossing the legs.
- Quiet, meditative music, which has healing qualities, helps the relaxation of the receiver.
- Use a blanket and put a fresh tissue over the eyes.
- Begin with making the connection between you and the universal life energy, so that you can function as a healing channel.
- Stroke the aura three times to smooth it (from the head to the feet, elliptically). This is relaxing. However, be careful to move your arm close to your body when you go from the feet back to the head, as you will otherwise stroke against the aura.
- Sit comfortably and relaxed.
- Apply your hands without pressure, slightly arched, matching the shape of the body, so that you make good contact.
- It is very helpful for the receiver if you feel or breathe into the parts that you touch.
- Keep the contact between the hands and the body after the treatment has begun, even when changing into the next position. Do not remove your hands from the person without first telling them.

- Keep your fingers close together.
- It does not mean that Reiki is not flowing if your hands don't always feel "hot." The energy flow depends on the needs of the receiver. It absorbs as much energy as it needs. This can vary from session to session.
- Sometimes the receiver falls asleep during the treatment. This is actually an advantage, because the energy can flow freely without being consciously influenced.
- If organs or limbs are missing, give Reiki in these areas as if they were there. For example, treat an artificial limb and the remaining stump.
- In case of a cast, put your hands on it. Reiki flows through the cast.
- In case of burns, hold your hands over the injured area with some distance.
- It is recommended to let the receiver know that conditions can increase sometimes after the first Reiki treatment due to possible self–healing reactions and emotions. However, these feelings will in general pass within 12 to 24 hours.
- Before you reach the end of a session, ask the receiver if there is a place that still wants to be treated.
- To finish a session, put your hands in the arch of the knees and on the feet (fingertips touch tips of the toes) to become grounded.
- Apply a hand on the back and stroke the aura smooth three times. It is also possible to draw a line of energy from the posterior to the head. Afterwards express your thanks to the Universal Source.
- Think of Reiki in emergencies and accidents. Your hands are always ready to heal.

The key word for Reiki is simplicity. Let Reiki flow from your inner self. Be in your heart. Reiki will intuitively lead you to the places that need energy. Don't necessarily feel bound to the taught hand positions. Reiki will develop your inner knowledge. Follow the lead of your hands. Reiki will lead you.

Reiki energy is within you,
The Divine is the origin and the source.
You are connected to the source.
Reiki is unconditional love.

10

SPECIAL PERCEPTIONS AND REACTIONS DURING REIKI TREATMENTS

Reiki energy refines and increases our perceptions and sensibilities. Sometimes we may have special sensations during a treatment, and some realizations about the client may be transmitted to us. Reiki intuitively leads us to the places that require special attention. This makes it possible to not only treat the visible symptoms, but to reach the actual origin of an ailment.

Reactions can occur both in the person giving Reiki and in the receiver. The person who is acting as the Reiki channel is also charged with this energy during the treatment and is flooded with healing energy. At this point it is possible for the giver to perceive the following sensations: strong warmth or heat in the hands, tingles, vibrations, shaking (at times like electric waves), heat in the entire body, as well as sweat in certain places that become very hot and thus draw in a lot of energy. The energy runs in waves and little by little in cycles. Each cycle can endure several minutes, during which the hands stay on that particular spot until the "drawing in" of energy loosens up. If it feels as if the hands are glued to the spot, then they should definitely stay there longer, which can mean between 10 and 20 minutes. We know from ourselves and some other people, who, similar to an electrical transformer, alter energy and have reactions such as yawning, coughing, belching, hiccups, strong vibrating and shaking of the hands, thirst, etc. when they reach interrupted or blocked areas. We recommend that people who have these or similar reactions while giving Reiki try to not suppress these sensations, but to allow them.

If the Reiki receiver starts to cry or laugh during the treatment, it is important to stay with the area that released this emotion until calming sets in. The same is true for heat sensations. In these cases as well, one treats in the corresponding positions until they are normalized. In cases of cold sensations, it may be necessary to give Reiki longer and more often, as there could be a chronic problem in these areas.

In the Reiki receiver, the following sensations and reactions are possible: pressure in the head, stings, which suddenly run through the body (such as a twitch in the leg), feelings of heat or cold, which can be felt differently between the giver and receiver, emotions, such as laughing or crying, sightings of light and colors, pictures and visions.

Possible self-healing reactions of the receiver after the treatment could be: slight shivers, which will change into a nice feeling of warmth after about 10 minutes, the urgent need to use the bathroom, hunger or thirst, chronic ailments may become apparent, headaches, pressure in the head, emotions (usually after the 3rd treatment), a change in the condition of the stool and urine (Detoxification! Drinking a lot of water supports this process), intensifying of pain, for example with broken bones. It is common in a natural healing process for symptoms to increase first. These self-healing reactions usually pass within 12 to 24 hours. Sometimes it is necessary for the problems to pass the peak before they can leave the body completely.

After several Reiki sessions—the number is individually different—one feels "born again," full of energy, charged, free of pain, in harmony, relaxed, strengthened, balanced, full of joy and fresh courage to change things in one's life.

REIKI TREATMENT
Stroking the aura smooth

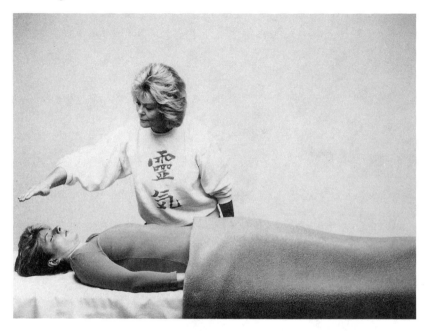

In the beginning of the treatment, you can smooth the aura (the energy field surrounding the body) with strokes following an oval shape from the head to the feet. This is very relaxing. Please be aware that your hands stay close to your body as you move them from the feet up to the head.

HEAD POSITION: H

H1—Eyes/sinuses

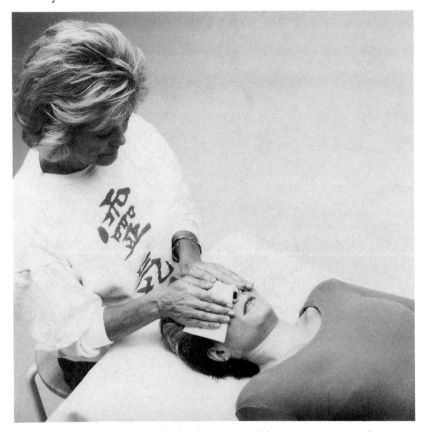

Over the forehead, eyes and cheeks. Eye problems • cataract • glaucoma • sinuses • colds • allergies • nerves in the brain • pituitary gland • pineal gland. Balances pituitary and pineal gland. Pituitary gland is the center of hormonal regulation. Relaxing in cases of stress and tightness. 6th chakra (third eye), is connected to the 1st chakra.

HEAD POSITION: H
H 2A—To the sides of the temples

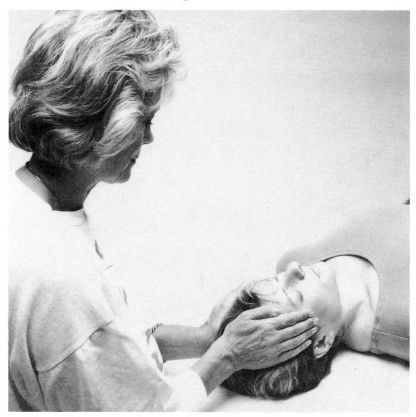

To the sides of the temples. Optic nerves. Balances the right (intuition, wisdom) and the left (rational understanding) sides of the brain. Very relaxing in cases of stress.

HEAD POSITION: H
H 2B—Ears

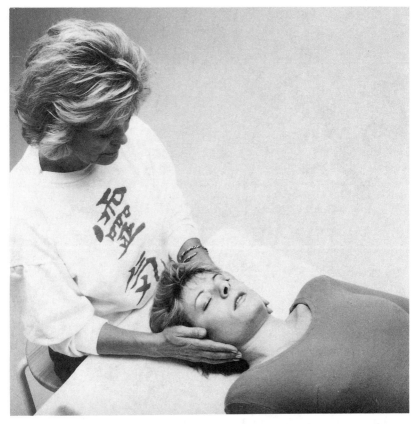

Over the ears. Treatment on the ears covers many organs (acupuncture points include heart, intestines, kidneys, lungs, stomach, liver, gall and others). In cases of colds and flu, lack of hearing, sounds in the ear, problems of balance.

HEAD POSITION: H
H 3—Back of the head

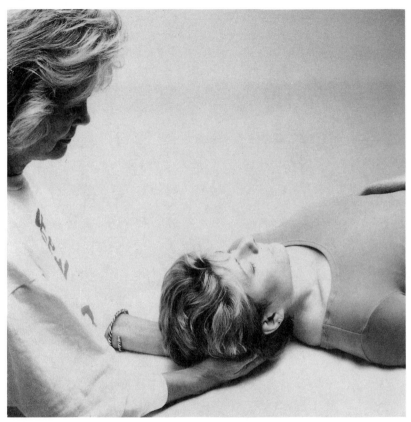

Back of the head, fingertips on Medulla Oblongata. Eyes • vision • headaches • nose bleeds • hay fever • sinuses • stroke • digestive problems fear • shock • worries. Calms and clears thoughts. Medulla Oblongata is connected to the third eye.

HEAD POSITION: H
H 4—On the top of the head

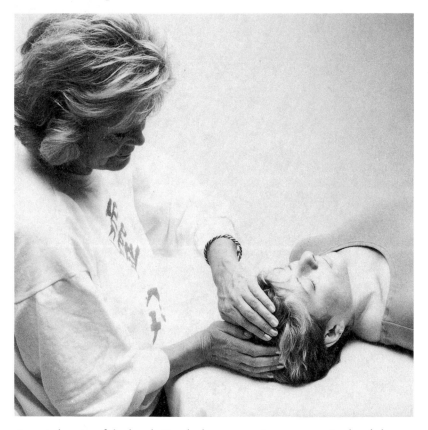

Across the top of the head. Headaches • eye pains • cramps in the abdomen • gas and digestive problems • bladder • multiple sclerosis • stress and emotions. 7th chakra.

HEAD POSITION: H
H 5—Thyroid gland/Thymus gland

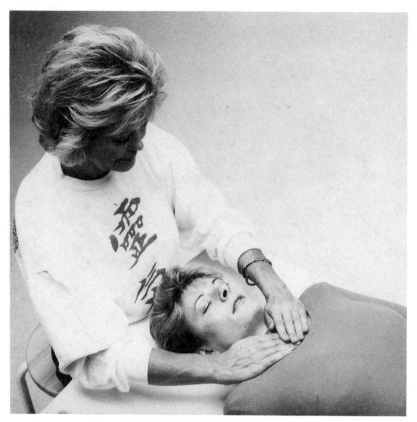

On the sides and front of the throat. Thyroid gland • important for metabolism • over or underweight • heart pounding and fluttering • sore throat • flu • high or low blood pressure • anger • frustration • communication • self expression. 5th chakra, connected to the 2nd chakra.

HEAD POSITION: H

Special Position—Eyes

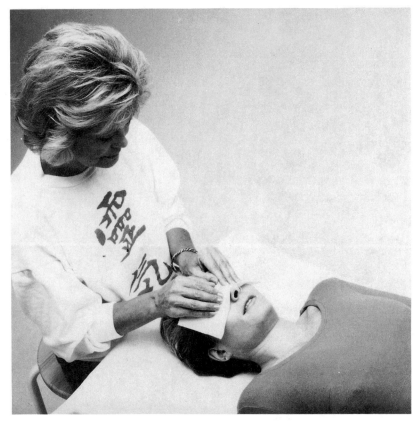

On the eyes. Putting the fingertips very softly on the eyes.

HEAD POSITION: H
Special Position—Eyes

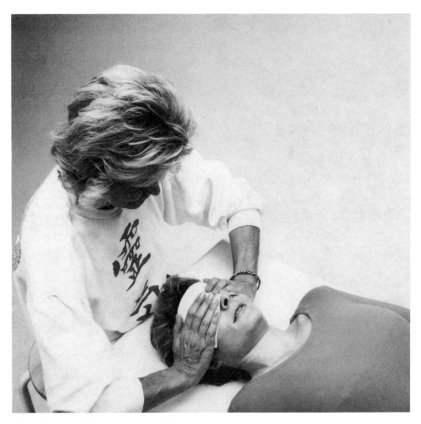

On the eyes. Eye nerves • sinuses.

HEAD POSITION: H
Special Position—To center

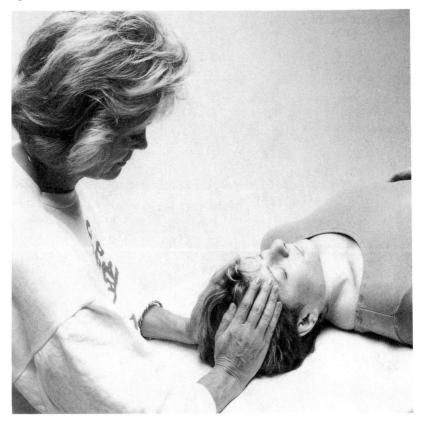

Sylvan fissure/capillary system. In cases of stress • tightness and headaches
• to center • balance problems.

HEAD POSITION: H
Special Position—Motor Nerves

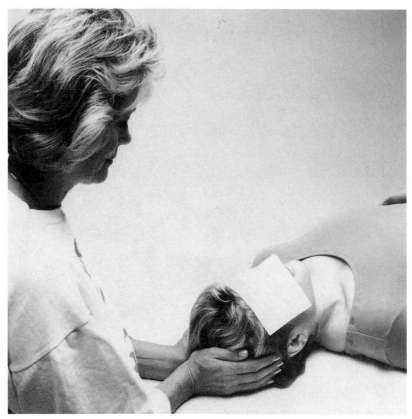

Motor Nerves.

HEAD POSITION: H
Special Position—Collarbone

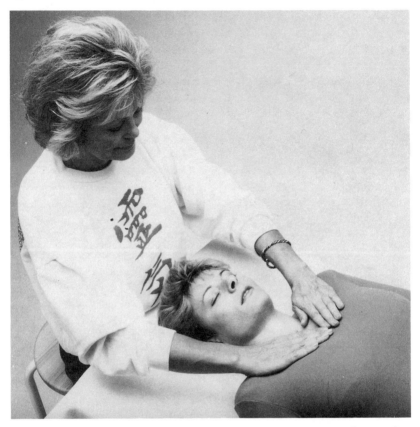

On the collarbone. Bronchial tubes • stress • emotions • asthma • fear • coughing.

HEAD POSITION: H
Special Position—Shoulders

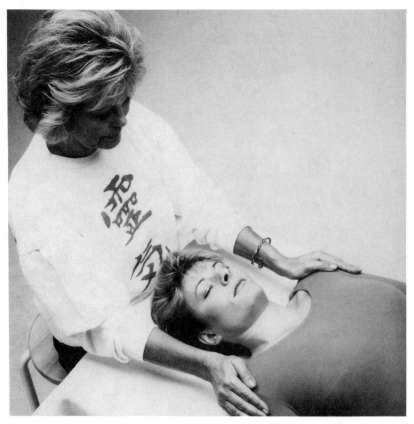

On the shoulders. Pains in the arms • cold hands • disrupted blood flow in the arms.

Basic Position (front): BP
BP 1—right, Liver / Gallbladder

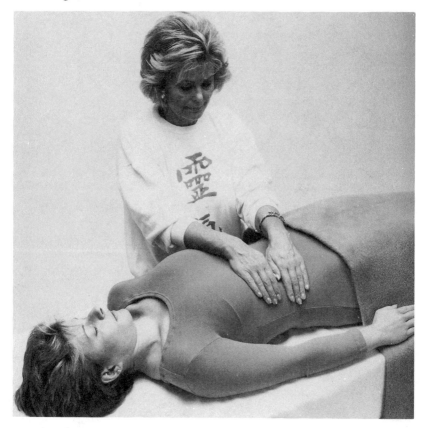

On the right, under the chest/waist. Liver • gallbladder • part of the stomach • pancreas • duodenum • large intestine • jaundice • gall stones • hypoglycemia • diabetes • detoxification • sadness • anger • depression • suppressed chronic illnesses • problems of balance.

Basic Position (front): BP
BP 2—left, Pancreas

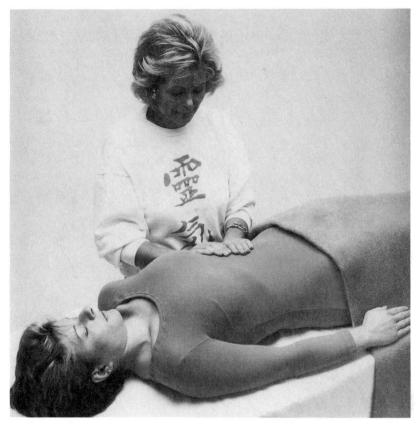

On the left, under the chest/waist. Parts of the stomach • tail of the pancreas (production of insulin and enzymes) • spleen • large intestine • small intestine • anemia • leukémia • immune system • diabetes • flu infection • Aids • cancer.

BASIC POSITION (FRONT): BP

BP 3—Solar plexus

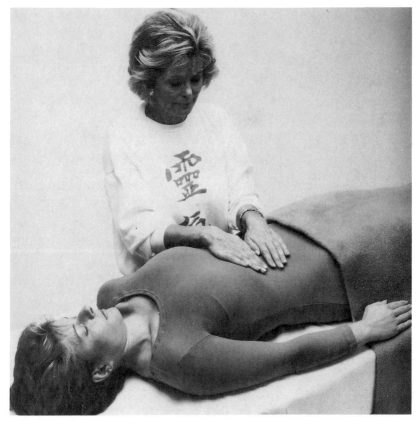

Lower hand on the navel, upper hand on the stomach. Solar plexus
• stomach • intestines • heart • digestion • lymph • shock • emotions
• depression • Hara, approximately 1 inch under the navel. 3rd chakra.

BASIC POSITION (FRONT): BP
BP 4—V–Position, abdomen

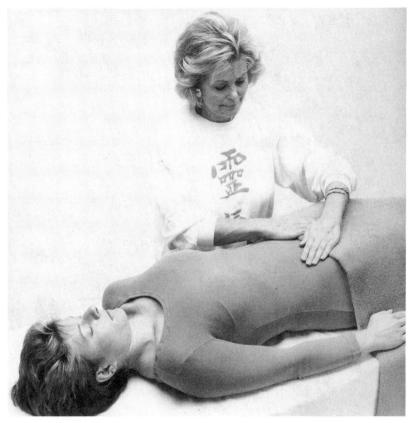

On the abdomen, V–Position. Organs in the abdomen • intestines • ovaries • bladder • urethra • blood circulation • digestion • appendix on the right • breast tumors • cramps • menopausal complications • back aches • tumors in the ovaries/uterus/bladder. 1st and 2nd chakra.

BASIC POSITION (FRONT): BP
BP 5—Heart/thymus

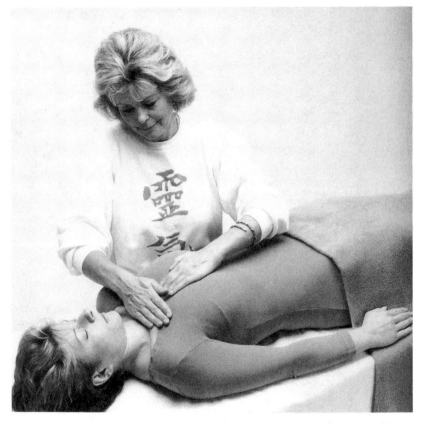

Heart, T–Position. Heart • thymus gland • lungs • heart problems • bronchitis • immune system • lymph • deafness • emotions. 4th chakra.

SPECIAL POSITIONS

Special Position—Greater Trochanter • Legs/Gall Bladder

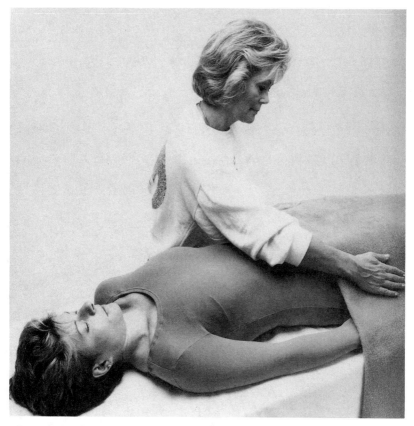

Greater Trochanter. Varicose veins • leg pains • gall point.

SPECIAL POSITIONS
Special Position—Breasts

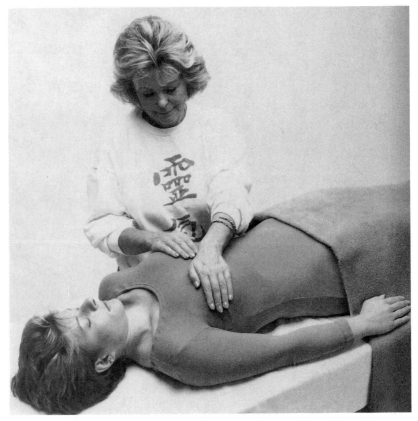

On both breasts. Harmonization of the masculine and feminine sides.

BACK POSITION: B

For B 1—B 6: Both hands together or next to each other, beginning on the shoulders, down to the edge of the buttocks.

B 1—Shoulders

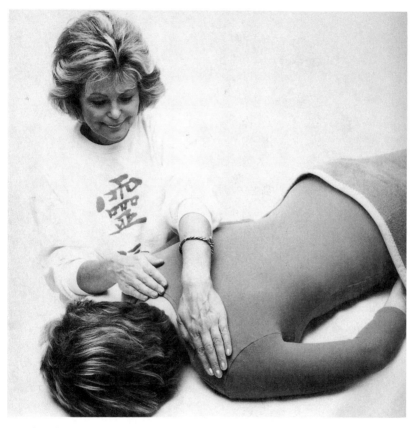

On the shoulders. Left and right on the shoulders • in cases of stress and tightness.

Back Position: B

For B 1—B 6: Both hands together or next to each other, beginning on the shoulders, down to the edge of the buttocks.

B 1A—7th vertebrae/Medulla Oblongata

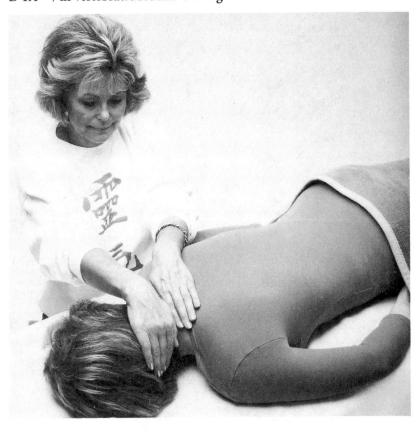

On the neck/7th vertebrae (Medulla Oblongata). For pain in bones • heart • vertebrae • nerves • shock on the spine • neck problems.

BACK POSITION: B

For B 1—B 6: Both hands together or next to each other, beginning on the shoulders, down to the edge of the buttocks.

B 2—Lung

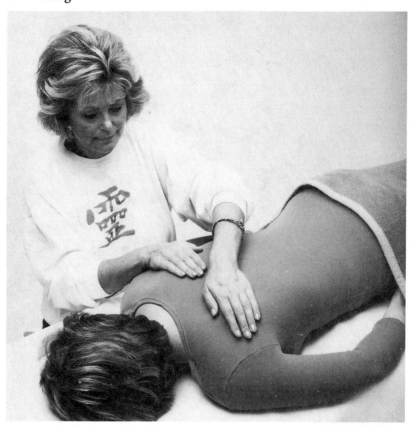

Over the lung. Coughing • bronchitis • stress • neck problems • back and shoulder complications • and as on the front of the body.

BACK POSITION: B

For B 1—B 6: Both hands together or next to each other, beginning on the shoulders, down to the edge of the buttocks.

B 3 and B 4—Kidneys (adrenal glands)

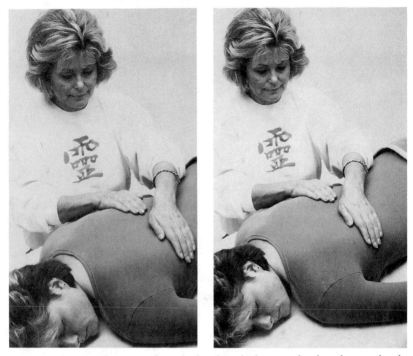

Nerves • heart • lung • adrenal glands • kidneys • back aches • shock • allergies • hay fever • stress • detoxification • in cases of emergencies and accidents • and as on the front of the body.

BACK POSITION: B

For B 1—B 6: Both hands together or next to each other, beginning on the shoulders, down to the edge of the buttocks.

B 5 and B 6—Hip/buttocks

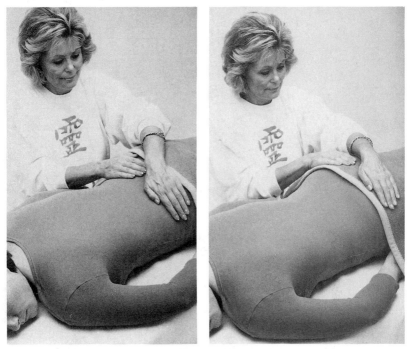

Sciatica • lymph • nerves • back aches • hip • and as the on the front of the body.

BACK POSITION: B

B 7—T–Position

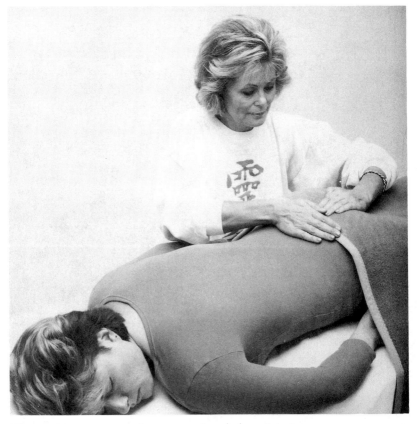

The energy center on the coccyx, 1st chakra. Sciatica • nerves • prostate • vaginal complications • bladder • hemorrhoids • and as on the front of the body.

BACK POSITION: B
B 8—Arch of the Knees

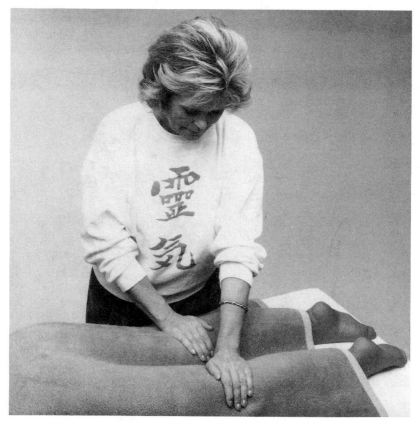

In the arch of the knees.

Back Position: B

B 9—Feet

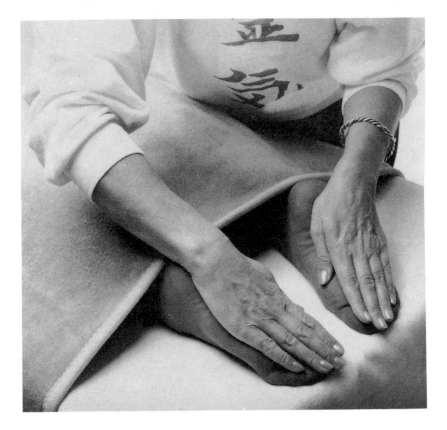

Bottom of the feet to get grounded. The fingertips touch the tips of the toes (end–position).

BACK POSITION: B
Special Position—Sciatica

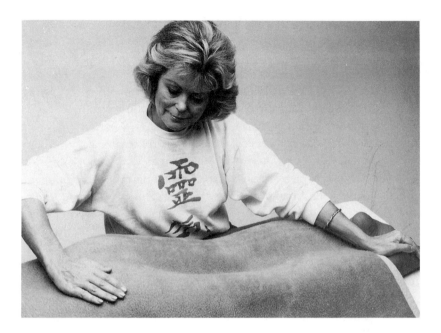

In case of sciatica pain, put one hand on the affected side of the buttocks, and the other on the heel of the foot of the same side. Also treat the entire leg from top to bottom.

12

First Aid with Reiki

It goes without saying that a medical doctor should always be called in cases of emergencies and accidents. But we can stay with an injured person, giving support and calmness with our Reiki hands until help arrives.

Because the injured person will in most cases be in shock, it is generally best to apply the hands onto the solar plexus or the suprenal gland. It is also possible to make a connection between the front and the back. In this case one's hand would be applied on the solar plexus and the other onto the suprenal gland. This brings back the innate Healer and will ease the shock. Later the outer shoulders could be treated. If the circumstances don't allow this sort of treatment then apply one hand onto the back of the head (Medulla Oblongata) and the other onto the forehead (forehead chakra). Otherwise simply hold one or both of the person's hands; Reiki will always flow!

Those trained in First Aid should take care of the necessary treatment. Reiki will automatically flow with this treatment, and the Reiki First Aid positions can be used in addition.

We have given First Aid with Reiki on numerous occasions and have always been surprised and delighted by how wonderfully the injured person was able to calm down.

There can always be situations where one is in a remote area where there is no medical aid available (during trips into the wilderness for instance). Here Reiki will always be ready to use, and it should be used repeatedly and for longer periods depending on how severe the injury is. In cases of poisoning through insects or snakebites it will be necessary to give Reiki with the appropriate emergency treatment for several hours without interruption so that the poison can be eliminated from the body.

THE FOLLOWING ARE SUGGESTIONS FOR FIRST AID WITH REIKI.

Fear	Hands on the solar plexus, adrenal glands and the back of the head. Also mental treatment with the 2nd grade.
Stroke	Immediately call a physician. Until a physician arrives apply hands onto the upper and lower stomach, not directly onto the heart.
Insect Bites	Directly onto the bite for 20 to 30 minutes. No swelling will occur if Reiki is given immediately.
Broken Bones	Bones should be set by a doctor before Reiki is given. Hands can be applied directly onto the cast.
Bruises	Immediately apply hands directly onto the bruise for 20 to 30 minutes.
Shock/Accident	Immediately call a physician. Until the physician arrives apply hands onto the solar–plexus and/or the adrenal glands. Later onto the outer shoulders.
Burns	Apply Reiki onto the injured area from a distance, for 20 to 30 minutes, possibly in intervals. Pain may increase at first, but will then recede. Blisters can be avoided if Reiki is given immediately.
Sprains	Apply Reiki onto the sprain for 30 to 60 minutes depending on the degree of the sprain. Repeat several times.
Wounds	Onto the injury, perhaps in intervals. Later onto the bandage.

Depending on the degree of the injury it is advisable to see a physician. Reiki will always support the positive aspect of any treatment and further healing.

13

SHORT REIKI TREATMENTS

The short Reiki treatment can be used anywhere, anytime, if someone does not feel well or is exhausted and in need of an energy charge. It is also very helpful in cases of stress and headaches. We let the Reiki receiver rest comfortably in a chair. Make sure that legs are not crossed or the hands folded, as this could block the energy flow.

We begin by placing our hands in the following positions:

1. First onto the shoulders.

2. Then onto the top of the head—do not touch the crown chakra directly—that is, leave space in between the hands. Also you may touch the sides of the head.

3. After this we put one hand onto medulla oblongata, the other over the forehead.

4. Followed by one hand on the 7th vertebrae (the prominent), and the other onto the throat.

5. Then one hand on the sternum/heart-center (between the breasts) and the other hand on the back.

6. Followed by the solar plexus (stomach) and the back.

7. Finally onto the lower stomach and the back down to the tail bone.

A short Reiki treatment like this harmonizes the chakras as we touch each area consecutively.

14

HARMONIZING THE CHAKRAS WITH REIKI

Harmonizing the chakras with Reiki is very effective. It can either be included in a complete treatment or be done separately if there is not enough time for a complete treatment. We can establish a good energy flow in only 20 minutes.

The chakras can be harmonized in various ways:

1. The chakras are harmonized with each other. Apply one hand on the 1st chakra (root chakra on the front of the body) and the other on the 6th chakra (forehead chakra). Feel the energy and wait until the same energy is sensed in both chakras. (Usually the root chakra feels cold and the forehead chakra is hot. Wait until both chakras feel the same temperature, although it is not an actual temperature—it is the way the energy is perceived). Now proceed with the other chakras in the same way. Following is the 2nd chakra (sacred chakra) with the 5th chakra (throat chakra), then the 3rd chakra (solar plexus) with the 4th chakra (heart chakra). Let intuition be the guide. Variations are possible, for example, the 2nd chakra could need harmonizing with the 4th chakra. The usual order is:

> 1st chakra with the 6th chakra
>
> 2nd chakra with the 5th chakra
>
> 3rd chakra with the 4th chakra or the 6th chakra
>
> 1st chakra with the 4th chakra
>
> 2nd chakra with the 4th chakra.

Because the chakras are in relation to each other—the 1st with the 6th, the 2nd with 5th, and the 3rd with the 4th—it is important to harmonize them.

For example, in cases of bladder problems, harmonize the 1st chakra with the 6th chakra. The bladder relating acupuncture points on the forehead also conduct the energy.

2. The chakras can also be harmonized or balanced by keeping one hand on the 1st or the 6th chakra while all other chakras are harmonized with it. This is done the following way: One hand is applied to the 1st chakra (root), the other on the 6th chakra (forehead). They stay in this position until the same energy is flowing in both hands. Then one hand is applied onto the 5th chakra (throat), while the lower hand stays on the root chakra. This is repeated with all the other chakras (4th, 3rd, 2nd chakras), and always until the same energy flows. If a person is very much "in their head,"—which is almost always the case—then it is best to start with the 6th chakra (forehead), then keep one hand there while all other chakras are consecutively harmonized with it. (Those who have received the Reiki initiation of the 2nd grade can also reinforce the harmonizing, or balancing, with the corresponding symbols).

3. Short Reiki treatments (see page 98) can also harmonize the chakras.

In general the rule is to let your Reiki intuition guide you. This may lead you to even more possibilities.

The Power Centers (Chakras)* of the Human Being

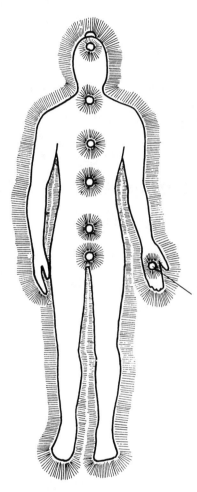

7. Crown Chakra

6. Forehead Chakra

   (Third Eye)

5. Throat Chakra

4. Heart Chakra

3. Solar–Plexus Chakra

2. Spleen Chakra

1. Root Chakra

Hand Chakra

---

* For further information on the chakras, we recommend *The Chakra Handbook* by Shalila Sharamon and Bodo J. Baginski.; also authors of the original book on Reiki: *Universal Life Energy.*

CHAKRA HARMONIZING (SELF TREATMENT)

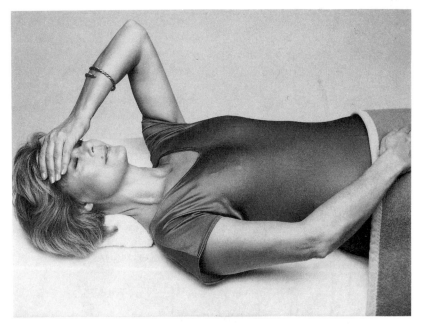

Balancing the Root Chakra (1) with the Forehead Chakra (6).

CHAKRA HARMONIZING (SELF TREATMENT)

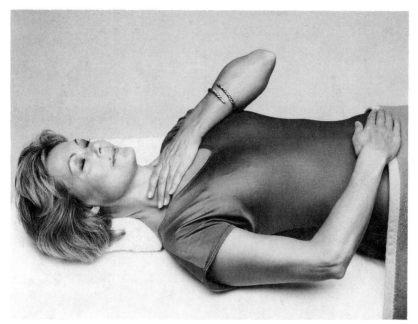

Balancing the Spleen Chakra (2) with the Throat Chakra (5).

CHAKRA HARMONIZING (SELF TREATMENT)

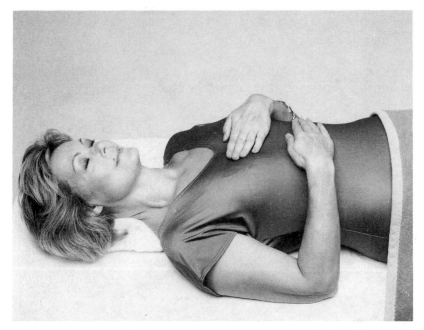

Balancing the Solar Plexus Chakra (3) with the Heart Chakra (4).

Chakra Harmonizing (treating others)

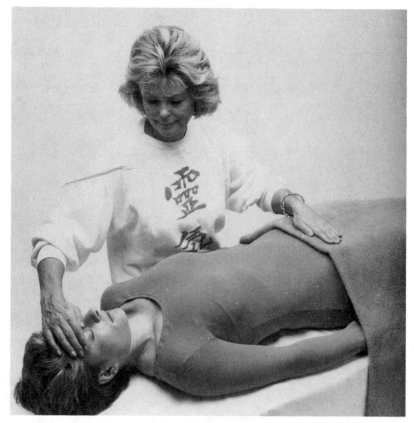

Balancing the Root Chakra (1) with the Forehead Chakra (6).

Chakra Harmonizing (treating others)

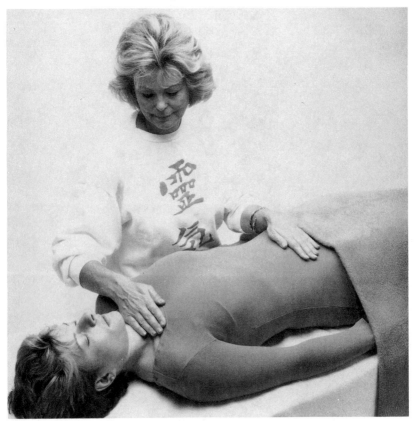

Balancing the Spleen Chakra (2) with the Throat Chakra (5).

CHAKRA HARMONIZING (TREATING OTHERS)

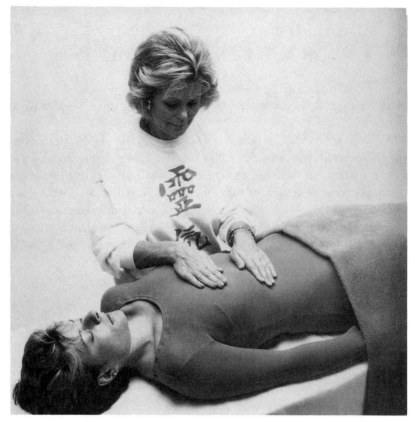

Balancing the Solar Plexus Chakra (3) with the Heart Chakra (4).

15

GROUP REIKI TREATMENTS

In meetings of Reiki practitioners, the high point is often a group Reiki treatment for everybody.

In group treatments, one person is treated by a group of Reiki practitioners. This generally happens in the following way: The group decides who will receive a treatment first, and this chosen person lies on a table, while the others place themselves around the table. A good way to begin is for the Reiki givers to form a circle around the receiver and hold hands to attune before the treatment begins. Now everyone finds a place for their hands.

We recommend to apply the hands in the following way:

- One person touching the head.

- Several people touching the organs on the front of the body.

- Maybe one person touching the insides of the thighs.

- One person touching the knees.

- One person touching the feet.

It is also a good idea to ask the receiver if the touch is comfortable (hands should be applied without pressure), and if there is a place which needs to be specially treated.

While the person is turned around onto the other side, it is recommended to keep the hands in contact with the body, so that they glide into their new position on the back.

When there are a lot of people in the group, a second or third tier can be formed. Those who can't find a spot directly with the receiver can put their hands onto the shoulders of the others and may form an outer circle around the group which is treating the receiver.

This type of group treatment has been used often and is always a wonderful experience for everyone present. Reiki energy is multiplied through the group and it should be noted that the power of the group energy sometimes leads to emotional reactions.

The following details should be taken into account for a balanced process:

- Everyone present should have a turn to receive a group treatment during the meeting.

- The room should be aired out before every treatment.

- A quiet environment should be created (no doorbell or telephone!)

- Quiet, meditative music supports the treatment.

- The receiver should rest comfortably.

- Conversations should be avoided during the treatment

- Choose a person for each treatment who will begin by smoothing the aura, will watch the agreed upon time for the treatment, and in conclusion will smooth the aura once more.

The time of a group treatment (with 6–8 people treating) will usually run 10 minutes each for the front and the back of the Reiki receiver, about 20 minutes total. If the receiver is still in an emotional stage (for example crying or laughing) at the end of the session, then the treatment should be continued until the receiver is harmonized.

16

REIKI TREATMENTS FOR EXPECTANT MOTHERS AND BABIES

Reiki shows a very positive impact on the mother and the baby if regular treatments (perhaps once a week) are started during the first months of pregnancy. The discomforts of these first months, such as morning sickness, depression, etc., can be eased.

The child will begin to kick and move inside the womb during a Reiki treatment of the mother. It is as if the child is happy! After a while it will calm down. Mother and child are in harmony. Of course the mother can treat herself anytime if she has received the Reiki initiation. We have been told that many strong babies, charged with energy, have been born. The mother should not participate in a Reiki workshop after the beginning of the 7th month of her pregnancy. Later she can treat her baby with Reiki, especially on its feet. The shock of birth will be overcome quicker. In any case, Reiki is always flowing, also when the mother is stroking her child or is holding it in her arms. Reiki can also help with any sort of complications the child may have. For instance, a three year old girl ran to her mother after she fell and hurt herself saying "Mom, please put your big warm Reiki hand on my arm."

We also know of cases where Reiki supports fertility. A woman who was unable to get pregnant for ten years finally became pregnant after her 1st Grade Reiki workshop. In an other case, a fifty year old man, who had tried previously to father a child, finally had success after the workshop. In both cases, wonderful babies were born.

Should the mother have health problems during her pregnancy, or perhaps even run the risk of losing the child, then Reiki can be very supportive in addition to the efforts of the treating doctor.

17

Reiki for the Dying

Reiki can be helpful when working with the very ill, infirm, or dying, as well as for their caretakers in hospitals or nursing homes. The caretakers are always able to recharge themselves with Reiki while they do their work, and this is an important prerequisite to being able to help others.

The uses for Reiki are countless in these situations. Beginning with holding a needy person's hand if they are afraid, or applying a hand on the person's shoulder, Reiki will flow with every contact. Ideally, a complete treatment can be given.

Reiki can be very calming and will help in accompanying people and animals while they are dying. It will let the natural process of dying take place, because Reiki is an intelligent force and follows the course of life.

The hand of the dying person can be held, or a treatment can be given to ease complications. This dying person will feel protected, and it will be easier to let go into the next dimension. Death in its literal sense doesn't exist. Birth and death are a transformation into a different form of being. The physical level is left behind. The soul, or our immortal essence, has slipped into a body during our lifetime on earth and will leave this body during the process of dying. "Dying is only a move into a prettier house" said the well known researcher Dr. Elizabeth Kübler-Ross in her book *On Life After Death*.

The following are some of the experiences we have been told about using Reiki in the care of the elderly or accompanying people on their dying journey.

> "In the course of our volunteer work with the elderly we visit many hospitals, nursing and caretaking homes. Often the poor people we meet are just miserable and confused, needing a helping hand. We have observed that when we let go of a person's hand, the other will spontaneously be taken, and the energy flows! This for us is a beautiful wonder which we are thankful to experience."

"My wife was suffering from cancer in its last stage. Traditional medical practices did not see any more practical options for treatment. Because of this, I decided to give up my academic skeptical attitude toward things outside of the scientific framework. I attended the next available Reiki workshop and received the 1st Grade.

My initial attitude melted during the workshop like snow in the sun of spring. Already, things were happening that I never thought were possible. Even the first shy attempts to help my wife during the workshop resulted in her feeling better and she told me 'I think you are able to heal.' At the end of the workshop, many of the other participants wished me luck for my difficult voyage. There also were some people who had experienced cancer with members of their own families. They warned me to be modest in my expectations, and to expect more of a relief from the complications than an actual cure.

However, my optimistic and energetic nature steered me toward healing. I immediately began giving Reiki at home during four consecutive days, and then in 2-day, and later in 3-day intervals. My wife felt better every time, and I realized what incredible amounts of energy were flowing in certain places. I was aware of what this meant. There were signs of hope, such as places that I had not touched, although my wife proclaimed that I had and that all the pain had disappeared. There were also discouraging signs, much like extinguished candles that could have burned much longer.

When my wife could not lie down anymore, I gave her Reiki sitting up. It was impossible to retain the regular positions, and I was forced to follow my own feelings and to develop new positions. When the touch of hands led to discomfort and even pain, I learned to work with the aura and got the same results as if I had applied hands. I had my wife tell me at what distance the power of my hands became uncomfortable, and made a note of how my hands felt at this distance. She was surprised when I was able to keep the right distance, which was quite different at different parts of the body, without her further instructions.

Metastasis in her lung caused strong cough-attacks, especially while driving in a cold car. Simply extending my hand in front of her chest was enough to stop the attack, and she would be free from coughing for half an hour. We called it "the cough drop." When her lung began to slowly fill with water, the coughing caused her to have great trouble while lying down and trying to fall asleep. I would greet her in bed with my extended hands, and immediately put one hand on the fear point on the back of the head (position H–3) and the other hand on the middle of the back, roughly in position B–3. She would fall asleep within five minutes. When this happened for the first time, she told me it was a wonder. She had never fallen asleep so fast, and she had never slept through the night so well. We kept this routine until the end.

We were both trained in meditation through yoga, books, and other workshops. We used meditation in such a way that my wife would try to reach complete stillness. Later we would both meditate before a Reiki treatment, and I would return from my state of meditation earlier than my wife and then give her Reiki.

We meditated long and deeply on the last evening that we were granted together. It was especially beautiful because, as it turned out later, a Reiki friend was giving us both Reiki from afar at the same time. With Reiki I had finally found the strength to say yes to the Father's request *thy will be done*. Until that day I had always had great difficulty with this request. Now Reiki's blessing stood behind my wife and I prayed humbly: 'Where I cannot heal, let me help. Where I cannot help, let me ease.' We do not give Reiki against God's will, but because of His divine grace.

We did not succeed in the cure of the cancer. My wife died peacefully and quietly the following night. She escaped a much more terrible fate, as she was threatened with a slow and painful death through suffocation. She went into death in such a quiet and fearless way that no traces of cramps were left. She smiled in her death. This is where the calming quality of Reiki is documented.

After my wife died, there were people who told me that I had not helped with all that Reiki. But I know that I helped my wife on her difficult path. It really depends on how it is viewed. A glass of water can be half empty or half full. The physical being is the same. At this point I would like to thank everyone who gave me the strength with distant Reiki to make it through those hard times. Also I would like to thank all those who cared for my wife, be it with or without Reiki."

*

"When we arrived in England last spring, my girlfriend's mother was dying. She was constantly vomiting, choking and was very nervous. I was alone with her and gave her Reiki for a few minutes. When my girlfriend returned, she was surprised at how quiet her mother now was. She had stopped vomiting and was resting in her bed. I gave her distant Reiki for one or two days, and she died very peacefully on the fifth day. I also came across difficulties and at times the light seemed to be far in the distance. However, I believe that I am also on the way to trusting Reiki, the godly love, 100 percent."

It is also possible to accompany animals in their dying process. We have had this experience ourselves with our dogs. We touched them with our hands and held them after they were put to sleep. We also helped them on their way by using distant Reiki.

This should encourage all animal lovers to be with their pet in the dying process—for example while it is being put to sleep by a veterinarian. This is the last rite that one can give a faithful companion.

The following is a Reiki friend's report on this subject:

"A friend recommended Reiki when I told her about my cancer stricken dog. I went to a Reiki workshop to help the dog, who meant a lot to me. I was in despair because I knew that it would die soon. I prayed to God and was not ready to lose my dog. Already on the first evening of the workshop, I gained what could perhaps be called a deeper comprehension. I experienced a wonderful development in the course of the workshop. I did not realize how much I had opened until I returned home. My dog could not greet me anymore, he was lying apathetically on his side. My mother told me that this condition had occurred only within the last hours. I treated my dog with Reiki for an hour, which he seemed to enjoy. When someone rang the doorbell, he jumped up, barked and wagged his tail to greet the visitor. My mother was completely astonished, even though she is very critical. Then the day came when I had to let my dog go. This day, which I had feared for years, went by very harmoniously. Although I was not able to let go of my dog's physical shell without any sadness—I am not that far yet—I was able to let go of him with only good thoughts. Today I think that this dog had fulfilled his task on earth by connecting me with Reiki. Although I now have another dog, I think that my first one was a special creature."

18

TREATING ANIMALS WITH REIKI

Animals like Reiki a lot. Especially our pets, such as dogs, cats, guinea pigs, hamsters and birds—but also horses, cows, chickens, sheep and pigs. Sick animals will like getting Reiki. Animals gratefully take the energy in, they are not disrupted by their intellect. They immediately feel that something special is coming from Reiki hands!

When treating animals, be aware of how they turn towards your hands. Animals usually show us exactly where they want the Reiki hands placed. If you move your hands, you can observe that the animal will turn itself in such a way that your hands touch the original places. The animal will also stay still as long as it needs Reiki, and this depends on how sick the animal is. Usually they can be treated for 20 to 30 minutes. Dogs stay still longer, while cats are very sensitive to energy and will jump away earlier. Very sick animals can be treated for one or two hours. They will let you know when to stop, either they will jump away or stand up.

The cat Maria Theresa was very sick when we took the pictures for this book. She had a cold, a sore throat, and was breathing heavily. Brigitte applied her hands for an hour, then the cat rolled and stretched itself. She felt much better. Her owner later told us that the cat had another attack the next day and was breathing heavily for about twenty minutes. She then gave her Reiki and the attack was over within twenty minutes. Twenty-four hours later the cat ate and drank for the first time in seven days. It was clear that she felt better. In cases like this it is advantageous to treat the animal every day for a period of time.

Also treat the organs which are connected to a given illness. For example, the spleen (immune system), kidneys (secretion), and head/throat in case of a cold. It is exactly the same as in humans. Long, daily Reiki treatments after surgery on an animal can accelerate the healing process.

Because Reiki affects body, spirit and soul, it is also very good to use on animals that have behavior problems or signs of abuse. Abused dogs and cats usually don't want to be touched at first. Later they feel Reiki's radiation and calm down quickly. It can be helpful to pet them and to talk to them. Reiki would be very supporting for veterinarians, animal activists and animal homes. Especially an animal's psyche reacts positively to Reiki. Often animals will lick the hands of a stranger who is giving them Reiki.

During workshops we are often told by participants that their animals behave completely differently after they return home. We have heard of dogs that were surprised, sniffed excitedly, and sometimes ran away. After a while they come back, want a lot of love and act frisky. Sometimes they will show the complete opposite behavior. A dog that wasn't very accessible before became very friendly. We have similar reports about cats. In the first night after the Reiki initiation they will lie on their owners stomach or another body part, and even come into bed although they may have never done so before.

If you are treating a larger animal, such as a horse or a cow, your hands can be applied right on the affected body parts; for example a lame or swollen leg can be treated directly. If the leg is bandaged, put your hands over the bandage, Reiki will go through. This is also recommended on the head and behind the ears. Horses will usually let their head hang in a relaxed way and begin to doze off (as can be seen in the pictures). The horse in the pictures is called Godiva and is ridden by Brigitte.

Distant Reiki treatments (2nd Grade) can be used with large animals living in the wild or with animals in a zoo. When we saw some whales that were in trouble on TV, we gave them distant Reiki.

While we were in the stable to take the pictures of the horse, a small kitty played with the butterfly in the picture. It was hurt and unable to fly. Brigitte took it in her hand and gave it Reiki. At first it was completely paralyzed, but then it began to move and we put it onto a nearby bush. It is also possible to breathe new life into birds that fly against a glass window. At one point Brigitte found a small hedgehog that had fallen into the drain of a swimming pool. It was completely exhausted, but after 20 minutes of Reiki it began to move and ambled into the garden. There are many opportunities to help our animals with Reiki.

FOLLOWING IS A LIST OF THE BEST WAYS TO TREAT ANIMALS:

Cats and Dogs
Behind the ears, one hand on the head the other under the throat; onto the chest, belly, back, hips and the organs. Also treat the pain areas, such as a wounded paw, directly.

Horses and Cows
Like cats and dogs, also horse's lame legs (over the bandages), on the head behind the ears and in the middle over the eyes.

Fish
Put your hands on the fish tank.

Birds
Hold the bird in your hand, or put your hands on the cage.

Animals in a Zoo and those in Emergencies or Catastrophes
If possible treat the animal directly, otherwise give distant Reiki (2nd Grade).

We have a special place in our hearts for animals. We have both had dogs and many opportunities to help them with Reiki.

REIKI TREATMENT OF ANIMALS

Godiva, a 16 year old mare.

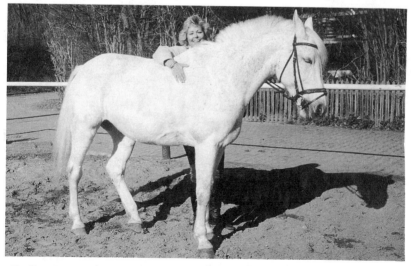

Godiva is completely relaxed when Reiki flows.

REIKI TREATMENT OF ANIMALS

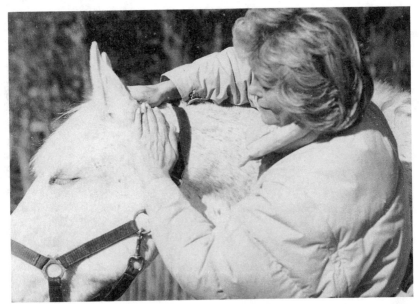

Godiva especially likes Reiki behind the ears. She is almost asleep!

In this position we treat a cold.
Godiva is very relaxed.

REIKI TREATMENT OF ANIMALS

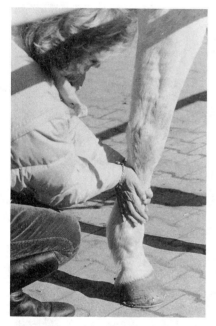

When the horse's legs have a problem, we hold them with our hands. This also works over a bandage.

This is the butterfly that we treated with Reiki in the stable.

REIKI TREATMENT OF ANIMALS

Danuta, a 13 year old Kuvasz, enjoys receiving Reiki very much. This position works well for arthritis in the joints.

This is how we apply the hands for problems in the hips.

REIKI TREATMENT OF ANIMALS

Reiki treatment for chest and kidneys.

Maria Theresa got Reiki on her chest for her cold.

19

Reiki Treatment of Plants, Minerals and Objects

Because Reiki is an energy that makes all life on earth grow and thrive, the results of Reiki treatments are especially visible in plants. You can even test this in the following way:

Plant some plants in such a way that you treat half of them daily with Reiki, and let the other half grow naturally, without Reiki. You will find out that the Reiki treatments will yield stronger plants.

When planting seeds, hold the grains in your hands for a while before you plant them. Give them Reiki every day while they sprout.

With young plants, simply hold them by their roots for several minutes.

With potted plants hold your hands around the pot and treat the roots. If necessary you can also treat the leaves.

With cut flowers hold the stems for several minutes, and later put your hands around the vase.

With 2nd Reiki Grade you can also treat your garden from a distance. A while ago we heard about a garden that was treated with Reiki from a distance and yielded a rich harvest of fruit while all other gardens in the area had a terrible harvest.

We can also especially help our forests with distant Reiki healing. And when you have a chance to be in a forest, you can hug a tree.

Minerals, such as crystals, precious stones and jewelry, can be cleaned or charged with Reiki energy. We hold these kinds of objects under running water for a short time and then hold them in our hands. Since matter is condensed vibration or spirit, it can be permeated by Reiki's energy.

We know from our own experiences and from numerous reports received over the years that:

- Car batteries can be recharged (please only touch the battery with gloves or give distant Reiki).

- The ignition system of a car was repaired.

- Jammed locks were opened.

- Vibrations in a room can be substantially improved or changed.

Sometimes situations are difficult to analyze, but remember, it is always a good idea to give Reiki a try.

20

Using Reiki for Food and Drink

We can also give Reiki to the foods we eat and drink, so they will be enriched with universal life energy. It really is a spiritual blessing of the foods. Since all matter has a certain vibrating frequency, we can increase this frequency through Reiki. For example, if we eat in restaurants a lot, we are able to change the vibrations of the food (it is always possible that the cook in the kitchen was in a bad mood, in which case that vibration would be in the food). We hold our hands over our foods and drinks inconspicuously and this allows a better digestion of the food. It is also possible to apply your hands onto your stomach after the meal.

We can also give our foods Reiki when we are preparing meals at home. Work with your hands as much as possible. Mix your salad with your hands and use them to knead dough or batter for bread and cakes. Everything that is touched with Reiki hands will receive this energy.

It has been reported that the taste of water or other drinks changes considerably after being treated with Reiki. This may be a good idea for an experiment.

Sprouts and seedlings which receive daily Reiki treatments will sprout much faster than those that don't. Try this yourself! Reiki improves the quality and nutritional value of foods and drinks.

The following is a story from a participant in one of our workshops, who owns a pizzeria, showing that the everyday uses for Reiki are limitless:

> "I was busy making a pizza in my restaurant, when I suddenly thought about my wife who was attending a Reiki workshop with Horst. Somehow I was overcome with the idea that I should make a *Reiki pizza*. I got into the right mood, treated the dough with Reiki, and gave the whole pizza Reiki once before I put it into the oven, and again before I served it.

When my guest—a regular customer—had finished eating, I went to his table to take the plate and asked, like I always do, 'Did you like the pizza?'

'Yes' he replied, 'but do you have a new cook?'

I said 'No'.

'Did you maybe use a new recipe for the dough?'

'No' I replied, 'didn't you like it?'

'Oh yes I did,' said my guest, 'it was exceptionally good.' He seemed a bit irritated and shook his head. 'If the cook and the dough are the same…, this pizza was good, exceptionally good… I mean I always like the food here… but this pizza, I don't know… this pizza was somehow *different*.'"

21

LONG DISTANCE REIKI OF THE 2ND GRADE

In the chapter "How to Become a Reiki Channel?" we explained the circumstances under which one can receive the 2nd Grade, and how it is different from the 1st Grade. An important aspect of the 2nd Grade is the ability to heal from a distance. It also makes it possible to transmit spiritual messages to reinforce the healing power.

The symbols that become familiar with the 2nd Grade initiation allow one to connect with the person being treated on the mental and spitiual level. In the same way we can connect with the divine power, beyond space and time.

It is also possible to give yourself a distant treatment. This way the higher self will treat the body, spirit and soul from within yourself. You will see yourself from a *higher place*. You can also treat your back, and can influence and change your thoughts in a positive direction through a mental transmission.

This process will transmit loving, healing energy over a bridge of light.

We ask for your understanding that we cannot discuss distant treatments any further at this point, because it is only possible as part of the 2nd Grade initiation.

22

THE UNIVERSAL RULE OF GIVING AND RECEIVING

For every Reiki treatment given, an exchange of energy should take place. By "exchange of energy" we mean that something should be *given* for the treatment *received.*

The simplest way for this to happen would be to exchange treatments, if both people have been initiated into Reiki.

If this is not the case, then a donation of money, gifts, flowers, theater tickets or a trade of other types of work can serve as an exchange of energy for the treatment. It is not the Reiki energy that is paid or traded for, but the *time* which the Reiki giving person made accessible. This person could have spent this time working for their livelihood, and thus should receive some kind of reimbursement. If the practitioner does not want the money for personal use, then it is possible to use it as a donation to charity or community organization. But those using Reiki professionally will need to be reimbursed for their time and they will charge a certain fee.

If one is not willing to receive something for a treatment, then it might be necessary to feel one's inner self to see if there may be a problem with receiving, or one's self-esteem. It could be that one awakens feelings of commitment or guilt in the other person, or even make him into the beggar (see Dr. Usui's treatment of the beggars, Ch. 2). The client should be given the chance to pay for his treatment. Through this, he will be freed from the weight of commitments and karmic responsibilities.

However, if someone wants to *consume* only, and does not want to *give* something for a treatment, then it could be that the person is not actively involved in the healing process, or possibly that the Reiki practitioner has a personal problem with the receiving person. This is why the kind and amount of the energy exchange should be discussed clearly before beginning a series of treatments.

The Universal Rule of Giving and Receiving stands in relation to the natural principle of resonance. There is much truth in old proverbs, for example:

> "What goes up must come down."

> "You reap what you sow."

> "Do unto others as you would have them do unto you."

In accordance to the spiritual rules, an exchange of energy has to take place to keep harmony in the universe. We would like to quote lesson number 108 from the Course in Miracles:

> "To give and to receive are one in truth."

Another example clarifies this: someone not willing to receive will disrupt the flow of energy, which is exactly as if one refuses to give. The cycle of energy has to be kept alive!

Life is a constant process of giving and receiving. After all, our life on this planet is a gift—and we are able to give so much. It is a constant allowing of the flow. Wherever there is flow or movement, there is life!

GLOBAL PEACE ON EARTH THROUGH REIKI

Peace begins with yourself. Peace of the soul is a personal matter. It has to start with your own inner thoughts and be extended outward. It is your inner peace that will create a peaceful world. With Reiki, you can feel your inner peace, be in harmony with all other living beings.

The following are some peace activities in which you can participate.

Global Peace on Earth with Reiki
Every Sunday from 9:00 to 9:15 a.m. Pacific Time.
—For all friends of Reiki—

Peace Clock, 12 o'clock Noon
Begin: Wherever you are, place yourself in a deep, quiet meditation for world–wide peace, everyday at 12:00 Noon for one minute. The goal is that on January 1, 2000, every human being on earth will take part in this meditation.
Further information:

> Peace Clock, P.O. Box 8307
> Calabasas, CA 91302, USA

Global Healing Meditation
Yearly on December 31., at 12 greenwich Time and on the last day of every month. For more information:

> The Planetary Commission for Global Healing
> c/o The Quartus Foundation
> P.O. Box 1768
> Boerne TX 78006
> USA
> Telephone: (210) 249-3985

The Planetary Commission is calling upon us to get together in thoughts during those days for a world–wide healing meditation. The first time this meditation took place was on December 31, 1986, and more than 41 million people participated. These numbers grew as the event took place in 1987, 1988 and 1989. More information is available in the book *Your Future is Now* by John Randolf Price.

INTERNATIONAL HEALING MEDITATION
by John Randolph Price

In the beginning—
In the beginning God.
In the Beginning, God created heaven and earth.
And God spoke, let there be light; and there was light.

Now it is time for the new beginning.
I am a co-creator with God, and it is a new Heaven
  that comes,
as the Good Will of God is expressed on Earth through me.
It is the kingdom of Light, Love, Peace and Understanding.
And I am doing my part to reveal its Reality.

I begin with me.
I am a living soul and the Spirit of God dwells in me, as me.
I and the father are one, and all that the Father has is mine.
In Truth, I am the Christ of God.

What is true of me is true of everyone,
for God is all and all is God.
I see only the Spirit of God in every Soul.
And to every man, woman and child on earth I say:
I love you, for you are me.
You are my Holy Self.

I now open my heart,
and let the pure essence of Unconditional Love pour out.
I see it as a Golden Light radiating from the center of
  my being,
and I feel its Divine Vibration in and through me, above
  and below me.

I am one with the Light.

I am filled with the Light.
I am illumined by the Light.
I am the Light of the world.

With purpose of mind, I send forth the Light
I let the radiance go before me to join the other Lights.
I know this is happening all over the world at this moment.
I see the merging Lights.
There is now one Light. We are the Light of the World.

The one Light of Love, Peace and Understanding is moving.
It flows across the face of the Earth,
touching and illuminating every soul in the shadow of
*   the illusion.*
And where there was darkness, there is now the Light
*   of Reality.*

And the Radiance grows, permeating, saturating every
*   form of life.*
There is only the vibration of one Perfect Life now.
All the kingdoms of the earth respond,
and the planet is alive with Light and Love.

There is total Oneness
and in this Oneness we speak the word.
Let the sense of separation by dissolved.
Let mankind be returned to Godkind.

Let peace come forth in every mind.
Let Love flow forth from every heart.
Let foregiveness reign in every soul
Let understanding be the common bond.

And now from the Light of the world,
the One Presence and Power of the Universe responds.

*The Activity of God is healing and harmonizing
   Planet Earth.
Omnipotence is made manifest.*

*I am seeing the salvation of the planet before my very eyes,
as all false beliefs and error patterns are dissolved.
The sense of separation is no more; the healing has
   taken place,
and the world is restored to sanity.*

*This is the beginning of Peace on Earth and Good Will
   toward all,
as Love flows forth from every heart,
forgiveness reigns in every soul,
and all hearts and minds are one in perfect understanding.*

It is done. And it is so.

23

Reiki Positions
for Enhancing Health

Reiki treatments can support any therapeutic treatment. We would like to point out again, that a physician should always be consulted before the treatment of an illness.

It is recommended to always give a whole–treatment, followed with concentrated treatments in the special positions for certain ailments which are explained as follows. In the case of emergencies or accidents, please refer to the chapter on First Aid with Reiki (see page 96).

> Head Position = H
> Basic Position = BP
> Back Position = B

ACCIDENT	As described under "Shock" and "Trauma." : B 3, B 4, adrenal glands and solar plexus, BP 3, in case of bleeding, hold directly over the affected area.
AIDS	TREAT EVERY DAY, especially H 2A, H 2B, H 3 and H 5, BP 1 and BP 2, especially spleen; BP 4, BP 5, B 3 and B 4 kidneys.
ALLERGIES	Sinus H 1, H 3, B 3 and B 4, adrenal glands, kidneys.
AMNESIA	H 4 and ovaries, BP 4 and prostate, B 7.

AMPUTATION	Treat the limb for blood circulation. In case of pain treat as described under Pain. Later put on the prosthesis and treat the bottom of both feet or the limb as if it were in place.
ANEMIA	Spleen, BP 2, left side, liver BP 1, from the side onto the head.
ARTHRITIS	Directly on the affected spots, such as front and back of the knee, B 3, B 4, kidneys. BP, R, especially kidneys, affected areas. Treat as described under Pain. Sciatica positions in case the lower limbs are affected.
ASTHMA	BP 5, also directly under the chest, collarbone. H 1, over sinus (lightly press a finger onto the sides of the nose–bone).
ATHELETE'S FOOT	BP and feet.
BACK PROBLEMS	BP, especially BP 3, BP 4, BP 5; B 1 to B 7, areas of pain.
BALANCE	BP 1 (gallbladder) and on the side of the head.
BIRTH	BP, especially BP 3, BP 4, BP 5, B, especially lower back. This will help open the pelvis, through which the baby attains a good position for a painless birth.
BLADDER	In general: BP 4, V–position, bladder and B 3, B 4, kidneys, H 1, H 4. Urine–Condition: BP 1 and BP 2, BP 4, H 1.

BLEEDING	BP 2, spleen, H, onto the head from the side.
	Menstrual Bleeding: BP 2, BP 3 and BP 4, H, onto the side of the head.
BLOOD PRESSURE, HIGH	H 5, 15 to 20 minutes, on the side of the throat, B 3 and B 4 over the kidneys and adrenal glands, under the arm pits.
BREAST TUMOR	BP, especially BP 4—15 to 20 minutes, BP 5 for some time, then over the tumor for 15 to 20 minutes, BP 2.
BREATHING	BP 5, chest, underneath the breasts and shoulder/collarbone. H 1, slightly press the sides of the nose–bone; B 2 and B 3 over the shoulder blades and over lower ribs to the right and left of the vertebrae. Feet, especially under the big toe.
BROKEN BONES	Let the bone be set first, then directly on the broken spot (Reiki will go through plaster casts).
BURSITIS	In general: BP, H, B 3 and B 4, over the kidneys.
	In the arms, neck, shoulder or chest: *Front*: Shoulders at the end of the collarbone near the throat.
	Back: B 1A, neck, shoulders.

In the arms, legs, or hips: B, next to the vertebrae and above the shoulder blades, both sides.

BURNS

Acute: Directly over the burn, as close as possible.

Not acute: BP and over burn.

CANCER

BP 1, BP 2, BP 3, BP 4, BP 5, all positions are important, solar plexus and over the area of the tumor.

Tongue Cancer: Under the feet.

Breast Cancer: BP 4 and BP 5 for a longer period of time, then over the tumor.

CIRCULATION

BP, especially BP 4, top of the shoulders, over the chest, above the nipples, rib cage, under the arm pits, inner side of the thighs, H, on the side of the head.

COLDS

BP, especially BP 5, BP 2, spleen, H 1, H 2B, H 3, also underneath the corners of the mouth (in case of throat pains H 5).

CONSTIPATION

BP, especially BP 3, BP 5, also simultaneously one hand over the navel and the other under the neck.

COUGH

BP, BP 5, H 1, H 5, throat, B 1 to B 4.

CRAMPS

BP, especially BP 4, B lower back, B 5 to B 7.

DEPRESSION	BP, H, especially H 3 and H 4 and B, especially B 3 and B 4, BP 5, collarbone.
DIABETES	BP, especially BP 1 (15 minutes), BP 2 and BP 3, over the navel, H, especially H 3, B 1, B 1A, B 2, B 3, especially in the neck on both sides of the vertebrae and B 7. Also the tip of the elbow, front of the shin bone, directly underneath the knee, pleura.
DIGESTION PROBLEMS	See Stomach.
DIZZINESS	See Balance.
EAR	Injured Eardrum: Middle finger into the ear opening, the others onto the head for 15 to 20 minutes; H 2B and behind the ears.
	Ear Pains: H 2B and BP 5.
	Deafness: Treat like ear pains.
ECZEMA	BP, B, especially, B 3 and B 4, kidneys and lungs.
EMOTIONAL UPSET	BP, especially BP 3 solar plexus and BP 4, BP 5, to the sides of the chest and in the line of the nipples, collarbone, H 2, from the side of the head, B, B 1, B 1A, B 2, B 3 and B 4.
EMPHYSEMA	BP, especially BP 5, collarbone, chest and back, throat and pleura.
ENERGY DEFICIANCY	BP 3 (over navel and Hara), B, B 7 and H 4, short Reiki treatment.

ENURESIS

BP, especially over the bladder (20 minutes), B 3 and B 4 over the kidneys and lower back, B 7.

EYES

For all eye problems: BP, especially BP 4 (for women), H 1—slightly press the fingers into the inner corner of the eye, against the eye ball and surface of the eye, also onto H 2A and H 3.

Cataract, cloudiness: Treat as above, each position 10 minutes, every day.

Squint-Eyes: BP, especially BP 4, as above.

Green Cataract: As above, especially ovaries, also H 2A and BP for 10 minutes (slightly press the tips of the fingers behind the jaw—bone directly behind the ear), H 3.

Chalazion Eye Sore: BP and H, especially H 1 and temples, back and especially kidneys.

FASTING

When hunger sets in: BP 3, BP 4, H 5, thyroid gland, B 3, B 4 and B 7.

FEVER

BP, especially BP 5, H, especially H 1 and H 3, slightly press fingers along the cheekbones, especially BP 1, BP 2, B 3, B 4.

FLATULENCE

BP 1 and BP 2, BP 3, H 4.

BRONCHITIS

BP 5, ribs directly underneath the chest and over the collarbone, H 1, press the sides of the nose, B 2, B 3, B 4.

FLU	BP, especially chest and breathing system, BP 1, liver, BP 2, spleen, BP 5; H under the chin, H 1, H 3, B 1 to B 4, B over and between the shoulder blades, under the feet, especially the big toes.
GLAUCOMA	See Eyes.
GOUT	Directly onto the affected spot, for example the knee, finger or hand, BP 3.
HAIR LOSS	BP, especially BP 4, B 3, B 4, kidneys and suprenal glands.
HAY FEVER	H 1, H 3, B 3, B 4, kidneys and suprenal glands, 20 minutes daily.
HEADACHES	BP, especially, BP 1, BP 3 and BP 4, H, especially H 1, H 2A, H 2B, H 3, H 4, B especially upper vertebrae, shoulder area, B 1, B 1A, B 2A, B 3, B 7.
HEART	Cardiac Infarction: Call a doctor immediately; upper and lower stomach, kidneys.
	Angina Pectoris: Especially BP 1, BP 2, BP 3, treat the diaphragm and body, thyroid gland, H, especially H 2, B 1 to B 4, especially upper back and adrenal glands.
	Stroke: Upper and lower stomach, kidneys, BP 1, BP 2, BP 3, B 3 and B 4.
	Cramp: BP, especially BP 5, under the chest, above the nipples, rib cage under the arms, H 2 to H 4.

	Enlargement: BP, chest above the nipples, H especially H 2.
	Pounding: BP, especially navel, thyroid gland.
HEARTBURN	See Stomach.
HEAT	BP, especially BP 4.
HEMORRHOIDS	B 7, over rectum (20 minutes), BP 2, spleen (15 to 20 minutes).
HICCUPS	Arms over the head, treat the diaphragm and the body.
HYPERACTIVITY	BP, especially BP 1 and BP 3, H 2A, H 3, on the side of the head.
HYPOGLYCEMIA	BP 1, (15 to 20 minutes), B over kidneys, tip of the elbows.
INFECTIONS	For infections of all kinds. Under the feet, especially in the middle of the foot, underneath the heal, also directly on the infection, BP 1, BP 2, BP 5, B 3 and B 4.
INJURIES	Directly onto or over the injured area.
KIDNEYS	BP, especially BP 1, BP 2, BP 4, BP 5; H, H 2B; B 3 and B 4, collarbone.
KNEE	BP, BP 4, especially groin area, Greater Trochanter B, especially kidneys, knee cap and inner side of the knee.
LARYNX	Over the throat.

LEGS	In general: BP, groin area and Greater Trochanter.
	Blood circulation: BP, especially BP 4, H 4, inner thighs.
	Swollen Legs: BP, H 4, B 3 and B4, kidneys.
	Pain in the legs: BP, especially BP 4 (very important) also Greater Trochanter , B 3 and B 4, kidneys and adrenal glands.
	Varicose Veins: BP, especially BP 4, H 2B, rib cage to the side of the chest under the right arm pit, directly onto the affected area.
LEUKEMIA	BP, especially BP 2, spleen, B 3 and B 4 above spleen.
LIVER	BP 1, back between the shoulder blades and below to the right.
MENSTRUATION	For complications: BP 4, lower back, B 7, H 3.
MIGRAINE	H 3, H 4, see in section on headaches, for women, abdomen BP 4.
MOUTH	Burned Tongue: On the mouth, under the tongue.
	Stomatitis: BP, under the feet.
MUCUS OBSTRUCTION	For example BP 3, stomach, bronchi, coughing, asthma, BP 5, pleura under the arm pits.

MULTIPLE SCLEROSIS	BP, especially BP 3; H, especially H 2A, H 2B, H 3, H 4, especially motory nerves; B 1, B 1A, especially above the neck and between the shoulder blades, B 7, also affected areas, for example legs. With two practitioners: One person at the head, one at the feet.
NAUSEA	Morning Sickness: BP 1, BP 2, BP 3.
	Motion Sickness: See section on Balance.
NECK	Ailment; BP, especially BP 3 and BP 4, H, especially H 3 and neck, B 1A, especially the neck/shoulder area and the 7th vertebrae.
	Pain: Outer sides of the upper–arms from elbow to shoulder.
NERVOUS BREAKDOWN	BP, especially BP 3, BP 4 and BP 5, H 2A, H 2B, H 3, H 4, from the side onto the head B 3, B 4, B 7.
NOSE BLEEDS	H 3, H 5 to release tensions, BP 3, B 1A, B 2, shoulder blades.
PAIN	In general: Over the area of pain, also B 3 and B 4.
	For all bones in the body: B 1A, 7th vertebrae.
	Hip or leg pains: Back, Greater Trochanter.
	Pain in the arms: Back, tops of the shoulders, shoulder blades, shoulders and arms.

Arm, neck and shoulder pains: Tops of the shoulders, collarbone at the shoulder, neck and shoulder.

Leg pains: Greater Trochanter B 5 to B 7, and directly onto the affected area.

PLEURISY

BP, especially BP 5, rib cage, under the arm pits, H 1, apply light pressure under the eye brows with your fingers, B 2 to B 5.

PNEUMONIA

As described in pleurisy; rib cage and back/lung, B 2 to B 5, collarbone and upper chest area.

POLYP (NOSE)

See description of sinus treatment, H 1, H 3.

PROSTATE

B 7; BP, especially BP 4; H 1, H 4.

RHEUMATISM

BP, B, B 3 and B 4, especially kidney.

SCARS

On the scar.

SCIATICA

B 5 and B 6, B 7, buttocks, back of the thighs, make a connection between the heal of the foot and one of the buttocks with your hands, BP.

SCOLIOSIS

BP and B over vertebrae.

SHOCK

Immediate Treatment: BP 3, solar plexus and adrenal glands together or one at a time, then outer shoulders.

Later,after the shock: BP, especially BP 4, ovaries/prostate, B 3, B 4, especially kidneys and adrenal glands; H, H 3, H 4.

SINUS INFECTION

BP, chest/bronchi and collarbone, BP 5, H, H 1, slightly press finger onto bone under eye brows and cheek bone, H 3, B 1, B 1A, neck/shoulder area.

Growth in the sinuses/polyps: see Polyp.

SKIN

Red or brown spots on the skin: BP 1, liver (15 to 20 minutes).

SLEEPLESSNESS

BP 3, H, especially H 1, H 2B; B 1, B 1A, B 2, around the waist, collarbone area.

SPLEEN

BP 2, left side and back in the same area, B 3, B 4.

SPRAINS

Immediately: On the sprained area for 15 to 30 minutes.

After 24 hours: BP and onto the sprain, also Greater Trochanter, in case of leg or ankle injury.

STINGS

Bee, Mosquito, Wasp: Treat the sting directly for 15 to 20 minutes.

STOMACH

BP 2, BP 3, H 2B and H 4, B 7.

Heartburn: H 3.

Digestive Problems: BP 3, BP 4, BP 5, H 3, H 4, back B 3 and B 4 kidneys, and B 7, outsides of upper arms.

STROKE   BP on the head at the opposite side of the affected area of the body, for example the right side of the head if the left side of the body is affected.

STRUMA   BP, especially, BP 4, BP 5, B 7.

SURGERY   A full treatment before and after the surgery.

TEETHING   On the baby's cheeks, the bottom of the feet.

TEMPER   Uncontrolled: BP 1, BP 2, liver, gall, spleen, BP 3, BP 5, H 1, H 3.

TENSION   BP, especially BP 3, BP 4, BP 5; H 1, H 3, H 4, on the side of the head.

THYROID GLAND   In all cases where a treatment of the thyroid gland is necessary, also BP 4 and BP 7, while fasting and in cases of adipose/anorexia.

TONSILS   Infected: BP, H 1, H 3, H 5, B 3, B 4, kidneys.

                      Chronic: Treat regularly.

TOOTHACHE   On the painful area, H 1, H 2, upper and lower jaw.

TRAUMA   As described under "Shock," and the neck B 1, B 1A, B 2 to B 7.

ULCER

Pylorus: BP 3, BP 4.

Duodenum: BP, especially below the waist, BP 3, H 1, slightly press nose bone where the cartilage starts.

Stomach: Outside of upper arms.

WEIGHT PROBLEMS

Adipose: Ovaries/prostate, BP 4 and thyroid gland, H 5.

Anorexia: Greater Trochanter and side of the hips, then fat tissue.

24

REIKI SUPPORTS
ALL OTHER FORMS OF THERAPY AND
ALTERNATIVE METHODS OF HEALING

In general, it can be said that Reiki will automatically flow into any kind of hands-on treatment. With Reiki added, the treatment will be enriched and supported, for instance in: Massage, Footreflexology, Lymph Drainage, Soma-Massage, Breathing Therapy, Rebalancing, Shiatsu, Rolfing, Acupressure, Acupuncture, Cosmetic Massages, etc.

Reiki is especially useful for all people in healing professions, because they will be charged along with their patients with every treatment.

Other ways of healing respond positively to Reiki: Rebirthing, Autogenic Training (A.T.), Yoga, Meditation, Bach-Flowers and Californian Flower Essence, Homeopathy, Verana Color–Foils, Prescribed detox and fasting treatments, Psychotherapy, Music Therapy, Crystals and Precious Stones.

The Verana Color-Foil system harmonizes wonderfully with Reiki, and we have had very good related experiences. Because of this we would like to look at this system more closely.

The Verana Color-Foil system helps the bioenergetic transformation of body, mind, and soul. The system was developed by Vera A. Suchanek and is based on 20 years of research and on the observation of cosmic energies and their observable influences onto humans, animals and plants. The colorfoils enable the intake of the vertical rays from the sun to the earth and vice versa. They assist in connecting with the horizontal waves for the transmission and reception of information, so that we are able to live in physical and spiritual harmony with the cosmos and nature.

Vera Suchanek says: "We live today in a time of major changes in the energies of the earth and the cosmos. Because we are a part of nature, we have no other choice but to go with the flow of these changes in order to survive. For one year I conducted regular long distance energetic checkups on the energetic changes every two hours. Later I developed a sensitivity which enabled me to immediately recognize any change. The changes in the atmosphere did not appear with regularity."

There are many different color–foils with different effects, for example in cases of cancer, multiple sclerosis, AIDS, etc. The foils are also individually and intuitively chosen and measured. They are made by hand, and their use is very simple. One looks through the foils for 1–2 minutes or carries them and the body responds to them intuitively (Address information about the foils is found in the appendix.)

25

KIRLIAN PHOTOGRAPHY AND REIKI

With the help of their high-frequency photography, the two Russian scientists Semjon and Walentina Kirlian succeeded, after many years of research, in showing the microstructural, bioenergetic radiation (aura) of the human body, leaves, or other objects to the human eye.

Today, Kirlian photography is used by many doctors and healers for energetic analysis (see Peter Mandel, *Energy Emission Analysis*) as a way to see bioenergetic disturbances early on. These disturbances include tiredness, illness, and changing moods in the energy body of the human being. An illness exists in the energy body long before it is physically apparent.

The following Kirlian photographs were made available to us by a Reiki practitioner. They show the bioenergetic field of a hand before and after a mental Reiki treatment (2nd Grade), which was carried out for only a few seconds on the head:

"The pictures shown were taken on August 2, 1989 at about 9 p.m. I took pictures over the course of several months, always before and after Reiki treatments. Most striking were the experiments I made with mental treatments of the 2nd Grade. The pictures were made within five minutes, as we had a color laboratory. Immediately after the first picture, I gave this person—a man—a short mental treatment (light and love) as he was standing up. The changes that took place in the second Kirlian photography can hardly be put into words. I repeated these experiments with the mental treatment several times, and each time I felt deep respect and gratitude for this wonderful power. Especially for the enormous energy of thought."

First picture, before the mental Reiki treatment (S 8–2 Ho20889)

Second picture, after the mental Reiki treatment (S 8–2 Ho 020889) The stronger energetic radiation is clearly visible.

Lord, make me an instrument of Your Peace.
Where there is hatred, let me sow love.
Where there is injury, pardon,
Where there is doubt, faith,
Where there is despair, hope,
Where there is darkness, light,
*   and where there is sadness, joy.*

O Divine Master, grant that I may
not so much seek to be consoled,
*   as to console;*
To be understood, as to understand;
To be loved, as to love;
For it is in giving that we receive—
It is in pardoning that we are pardoned;
And it is in dying that we are born to eternal life.

A Prayer of St. Francis of Assisi

26

MY PATH WITH REIKI

By Brigitte Müller, Reiki Master/Teacher

I found the purpose of my life in Reiki. I had said the prayer of the holy St. Francis of Assisi long before I was led to Reiki, and my prayers were heard. While traveling in the United States in January of 1981, I met the Reiki Master Mary McFadyen in Northern California. She just "happened" to pick me up from the airport. As we were driving in her car she told me about Reiki. I was listening with great interest. When I asked her whether I could have a Reiki treatment, she told me that it was even possible to transmit Reiki in such a way that I could have the healing power in my own hands. I immediately asked Mary if there was a workshop anytime soon. She told me there was not one planned, but she could initiate me alone, without a workshop. The next day she agreed to it.

I was staying in a small cabin in a forest near Nevada City. Deer were walking outside my window and I was far away from the busy everyday life of the world. It was a perfect place to receive my initiation into the 1st Reiki Grade. Mary explained the treatment, and we practiced on each other. Those were wonderful days, and I thank Mary so very much for bringing Reiki to me at that time. In the beginning I could hardly grasp that I now had "healing hands." I felt a lot of power and warmth in my hands and applied them tentatively on myself to try Reiki! At the same time I had a burning desire to give someone else Reiki. But for this I had to wait a while.

First I flew back to Los Angeles. There I rented a room from an 80 year-old lady, and after a few days, I had an opportunity to successfully use Reiki. All of a sudden I heard yelling from the kitchen. The old lady had put her fingers into the garbage disposal to free a stuck piece of orange peel. However, she had forgotten to turn off the switch first, and her finger tips had been cut by the blades. She was bleeding profusely, and I immediately put on a pressure-bandage and also pressed my hands onto the wound. To my surprise, the bleeding stopped very quickly. It was just like the moment when Dr. Usui treated his injured foot with Reiki to stop the bleeding. We drove to the hospital because the wounds needed stitches. Upon arrival I applied my hands again, and the lady calmed down quickly. A nurse instructed me to leave the room, much to the dismay of the old lady. She insisted that I stay with her because my hands "felt so good." This was my first Reiki treatment. Every day I treated her hand which, to the surprise of the doctors, healed very quickly.

A short while later I flew back to Germany. My parents received my first Reiki treatments. After a few self–healing reactions, they felt very charged. My bulldog Etzel also liked Reiki a lot. He would lie down comfortably, sigh, and snore when I put my hands on him. My mother wanted to learn Reiki right away. Also some of my friends wanted to receive the initiation after I had familiarized them with Reiki. I organized the first Reiki workshop in Germany with Mary McFadyen in Hamburg in 1981, and then another one in Frankfurt. I translated the workshop's lectures into German, which gave me an opportunity to gain workshop experience. After my 1st Grade initiation in the U.S.A. I felt right away that it was my calling to be a Reiki Master. I received the 2nd Reiki Grade during Mary's stay. At this time I was also in training to become a naturopath.

After I passed the naturopath exam, I contacted Phyllis Lei Furumoto, Mrs. Hawayo Takata's granddaughter, to ask about the Reiki Master initiation. I flew to the United States and Canada in January of 1983, and traveled with Phyllis for several weeks. She looked at my abilities very closely. We drove through the beautiful Canadian countryside. I met several Reiki masters, and everywhere we went I was taken in as family. We participated in some Reiki workshops and gave Reiki treatments. Eventually our journey took us to Phyllis' house in Canada. After three weeks, she informed me that she would initiate me as a Reiki master. I was overjoyed!

The time came on January 27. 1983. Mary McFadyen came to my initiation which took place in a small wooden cabin belonging to another Reiki Master. We had to wade through the snow and began by making a small fire.

The initiation was a very deep experience for me and I was very happy. That afternoon Phyllis began a 1st Grade workshop and for the first time I was allowed to give an initiation. I felt a great inner peace and gratitude that

I was allowed to be the instrument for this divine power. I felt the pulsating energy in my entire body and my hands were tingling and vibrating. I thanked God from deep within my heart for his blessing and his grace. We celebrated the day with our Reiki students. Phyllis had some wonderful plums in her freezer, and I baked a German plum pie with whipped cream for the occasion. We were all abundantly cared for on this day of my Master initiation.

During the following days I received further training, and we also had a 2nd Grade workshop. In the course of those weeks, Phyllis and I found a deep inner connection with each other. It was a very intense time, and I felt the need for a peaceful retreat to let the master energy settle. We parted, and I went to Southern California to the Self–Realization Fellowship in Encinitas. This community was founded by Paramahansa Yogananda, the author of *Autobiography of a Yogi,* which he wrote there. This was the ideal place to retreat. I spent wonderful days meditating and praying. The meditation garden with its beautiful flowers, whispering streams and a pond with giant goldfish, directly on a cliff over the Pacific was a refreshment for my soul. This was where I was able to prepare myself for the life of a Reiki Master. I could clearly feel the blessing and vibrations of the enlightened master Paramahansa Yogananda, and I was very grateful to be there.

After those days of inner searching I was ready to return to Germany and to realize my life work.

There was a lot to do. Since I was the first Reiki Master in Germany and only a few people knew about Reiki, I was really a pioneer. Workshops had to be organized; I would like to thank all those who supported me at the time and are still helping me now.

A new part of my life began, and my task filled me entirely. It is such a beautiful feeling to be connected with everyone in a workshop group, to see how we grow together and become unified through love = Reiki. I have had deep inner perceptions and experiences, especially during Reiki initiations.

During the years of being a Reiki Master, and through meeting all the people participating in my workshops, I have come to feel Reiki in my heart and soul. I would like to convey in words how I personally perceive Reiki. The Reiki initiation touches our innermost being. This inner being is the divine spark or the divine Self within us, our immortal essence. It is like a reunification with God's Presence in our heart. We are reconnected with our center of love. Our innermost essence is love, and it is always present. We are love! However, many of us have forgotten this. Now the beam of love flows through the entire being, and a jubilant joy fills us. The inner source, which may have been blocked, once again begins to bubble. Our heart is connected with our hands. The hands bless everything and everybody with love. Love is the strongest force in the universe. It is the binding force that keeps planets, stars, suns and our Earth on track. We can feel that we are a part of creation, and also that everything exists within ourselves, just like a drop of the ocean contains the whole ocean.

Through the gentle touch of our hands we transmit Reiki = love = light = Universal Life Energy. This brings us close to ourselves—we are once again touching ourselves. Our entire being is filled with it, and the light glows from our eyes, heart, hands and bodies. Because love has the highest frequency, we experience a transformation into this higher frequency. Love is light! We are light! When all of a sudden it gets brighter in us, our dark sides will also be revealed. Love = light = Reiki also shines light on the things within ourselves that we don't like to see very much and enables us to accept them with equal love. Being able to see or recognize yourself is the beginning of the change. We now have a key in our hands which lets us form our lives the way we like. Reiki helps us to find our blocks and obstacles. Because we apply our Reiki hands on our own bodies every day and let in more and more light, we become more loving, harmonious, balanced and understanding with our- selves and others. We begin to accept and love ourselves the way we are.

For me a time of inner growth began. I learned a lot from my students in the workshops, because we are all teacher and student at the same time. Everyone learns from everyone. We teach what we learn ourselves. It was a joy to see how the hearts opened and we were all unified in love at the end of the workshop. We are always connected with this vibration because love has no limits.

Reiki took me to many countries where I was invited to give workshops. I had the distinct wish to bring Reiki into the eastern European countries. Before I was initiated as a Reiki Master, Phyllis Lei Furumoto asked me: "Why do you want to become a Reiki Master?" I told her I wanted to bring the Reiki light and the healing power to Germany as a way to contribute to the unification of the German people, and all other people; to heal the wounds of the wars, as I had lived in the former East Germany as a child.

Because of this, my trip to Poland was an experience that I will never forget. At the time, the "Week of Healing and Holistic Being" was taking place in Krakow, which was the first official event of the kind in Poland. It featured lectures, discussions, free seminars and meditation workshops. Teachers from around the world had traveled to Krakow to take part in the event. The Reiki workshops were so popular that we could hardly keep up with the work. 270 people were initiated into the 1st Grade in only four days, which was a real transformation for me. During this time I had great support from some Reiki friends who had traveled with me from Germany, thank you! People were searching for peace and light so strongly that it was a great pleasure to see their change and their glowing faces in the course of the workshops. Since that time, I have trained and initiated a Reiki Master in Poland, so that Reiki can spread further.

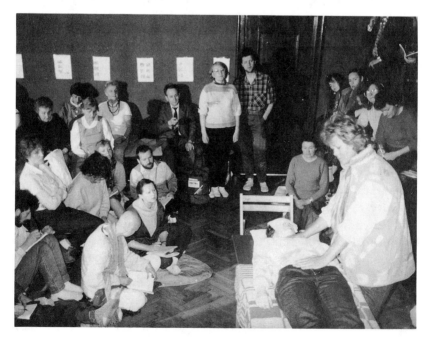

Brigitte Müller during a Reiki Workshop in Poland

Then, the Berlin Wall opened up here in Germany. That was a joyful day in my life!

Reiki led me into further self-discovery. Toward the end of 1983 I participated in a workshop with Elizabeth Kübler-Ross. This was very moving for me and I learned to take responsibility for my own emotions and experiences. I especially learned to be aware of unfinished business coming to the surface, and being conscious of people "pushing my buttons," or me pushing theirs. This often happens in workshops. I realized that the more clear I became with myself, the better I was able to help the people in my workshops.

During a stay in the U.S.A., I bought the book *Loving Relationships* by Sondra Ray. Reading this book and working with its exercises, I immediately saw my own "patterns," and I knew that I wanted to take part in the Loving Relationship Training as soon as possible. This training is about realizing the partly unconscious behavior patterns which are connected to the trauma of birth and childhood, and to transform them into self love and joyful, loving relationships. I participated in the training in May of 1986 in Stockholm and in November 1986 in London, and they were very revealing and healing for me. In the following years, I repeatedly participated in ten day follow-up trainings in Hawaii, the Bahamas and in Spain, and besides the group rebirthing sessions, I also received personal, one–on–one sessions. Reiki was very supporting in this rebirthing process. A lot of things were released and integrated within me. These workshops meant a lot to me, and have helped me to accept and love myself. I became more aware and began to watch my thoughts, because thoughts are creative! They manifest themselves. We ourselves create our circumstances through our thoughts. We can choose ourselves! This also corresponds with the spiritual rules of life. I remember the beggars in the history of Reiki, who didn't want to change their thoughts and perceptions of life. In the past we always looked for love, acknowledgment and peace on the outside, and now we are realizing that the source of all this is within ourselves: the source of divine love. In the moment that we are able to find love within ourselves, we become the masters of our lives. It isn't until that point that we can really love. We become free, we become love in action and won't need anything from the outside any longer—because everything we send out will return to us, this love will return to us many times over, eventually reunifying with the source, so that the cycle closes itself.

I have had countless experiences with healing forces in my years of intense Reiki work. At times there have even been spontaneous healings after one or two treatments. My hands have always been ready for immediate use, even in emergencies and accidents. On several occasions I was able to calm people after accidents, and relieve their pain and shock. Here are some experiences that I would like to share.

✳

The 83-year old husband of a friend got an infection and a painful enlargement of the testicles after a urethra examination. My friend, who is a 2nd Grade Reiki practitioner, began a treatment directly onto the testicles right away (if direct contact is not appropriate in your situation, give Reiki with a few inches of distance). I helped with the treatment twice a week. The doctors at the hospital decided that the testicle should be surgically removed, but postponed the operation because of bacteria in the urine. We kept giving intensive Reiki treatments. After four to five weeks the size of the testicle was reduced, and within four months the size was back to normal, making surgery unnecessary.

✳

When my male bulldog, Etzel, was about five years old he developed a heart defect, and the veterinarian prescribed an allopathic heart medication which I gave him every day for many years. After my initiation into 1st Grade Reiki, I gave him a lot of treatments, and we were able to slowly reduce the dosage of the medication. At a later examination by the veterinarian, no heart irregularities were detected, and the medication was stopped entirely. But when he was nearly twelve, Etzel became ill with leukemia. Again, he received many treatments from me and afterward, he always jumped up and licked my hands in joy. At times he got very weak, especially while taking walks. He would simply sit down and would not walk again until I put my hands around him. Soon after he would be charged again, stand up and jump around. If I removed my hands before he had received enough though, he would simply keep sitting. I stayed with him with, giving Reiki during his last hour, and his soul was able to peacefully change into another dimension. After his heart stopped beating, I held him in my arms for an hour and he looked as if he was asleep in peace. Reiki helped me stay calm during this difficult time. When my Mother touched my liver during a Reiki treatment on the following day, I was able to freely let my tears flow. A few months later I finished the grieving process—acceptance and integration of pain—in a workshop with Dr. Elizabeth Kübler-Ross. I thank you from the depth of my heart, Elizabeth.

✳

In the morning during a Reiki workshop, a lady who was taking part in another workshop at the center, injured her foot. She had landed on the foot in a bad way while dancing, and was suffering from a stretched ligament. Within seconds, two swellings the size of eggs had formed on the outside of her ankle. She was brought into our Reiki room with ice-packs on her foot. We immediately began giving Reiki with four to five people for several hours; head, front of the body, kidneys/adrenal glands, and directly onto the foot. I started out giving Reiki with the ice-pack on the foot, later I began alternately treating with and without the ice. Emotions were loosened, and the lady cried. We had also called a doctor to see whether the foot was broken. However, because we were on a 3500 foot mountain, the doctor—from the army—did not come until the evening. Meanwhile her foot was even more swollen and had become blue and green. It appeared to be going through an accelerated healing process. When the doctor arrived, he confirmed that her foot was not broken. He figured it would take two weeks for her to be able to put weight on the foot again. He also left some pain tablets, but she did not have to take them because Reiki was easing her pain. Even at night she did not have pain. The next morning we continued the Reiki group-treatment for about two hours. By the afternoon, the swelling had receded and all that was left was a small bruise around the ankle. In the evening at 6 o'clock, she stood up without crutches, was able to put weight on her foot and walked! Thirty hours had passed since the accident; that is how Reiki accelerated the healing process!

✳

During a workshop in Stuttgart, I was walking with a participant on the way back to the meeting room after lunch, when we saw a young man lying hunched up and motionless on the side of the street. With him was a large black dog on a leash. People were standing around him saying, "There is nothing we can do, it is much too late." We approached the man, got on our knees and began giving him Reiki. The participant put her hands on his kidneys, I put mine around his head without touching him. He smelled like alcohol and was not responding to my words. The dog stayed completely calm and looked on. After some time had passed, I put my hands directly onto his head. A few minutes passed and he gained consciousness. When I tried to remove my hands, he immediately said, "Please leave them where they are, they feel so good." We asked him if he was diabetic, but this was not the case. It turned out that he was epileptic and that drinking a beer had triggered the seizure. We continued the treatment. After a while he began to cry and sob, snuggling in my lap like a child seeking protection. He calmed down after about ten minutes, got up and was clear again. Meanwhile the police had been called. We asked for his address, so that his wife could be contacted, and when the police arrived, he was feeling fine. When we said good bye, he thanked us very much and told us that he was about to start an alcohol detox program. Once again the divine force was able to help.

The next important step on my Masters path was to undertake the training and initiation of Reiki masters. I felt deep within myself that the time had come, and felt ready when Phyllis Lei Furumoto gave me the blessing and empowerment to do so. At the end of 1988 I initiated the first Reiki master in Poland; more followed, and more are currently in training.

Being initiated as a Master does not mean that one has learned everything there is to learn. On the contrary, it is an admission into the higher knowledge of life. For myself it means to be ready for change, revitalize old ways of thinking, to receive everything with love and gratitude, to allow the flow of a higher force to transform energy, to be one with God's presence in my heart and to surrender to this guidance within.

My entire life and its quality has been changed by Reiki. Reiki is a wonder that shows me new wonders every day. My deepest wish is that many more people in the world receive the Reiki initiation, so that we can all come closer and become a large family living in peace, love and harmony on this earth. We are all one in spirit and in love.

I am thankful for God's grace and the blessing that I receive as this force works through me.

Brigitte Müller

27

MY PATH WITH REIKI

Horst H. Günther, Reiki Master/teacher

With gratitude and complete trust in the creativity of the universe, I want to begin this chapter with excerpts from the writings of the great physicist Max Planck:

"As a physicist, a man who served in the sober sciences and the description of matter for my entire life, I am free of the suspicion of being seen as a dreamer. With this in mind, I say the following as a result of my research of the atom: no matter exists by itself! All matter is created and exists only through the force which causes the vibration of the parts of the atom and which holds it together into the smallest solar system of an atom. Behind this force, we have to assume a conscious and intelligent spirit. This spirit is the origin of all matter. It is not the visible, transient matter that is actual, true, and real, because matter would not exist without spirit by itself. It is the invisible, immortal spirit that is real. But since the spirit cannot exist by itself, and since every spirit is part of a being, we must accept the existence of spiritual beings. But even spiritual beings cannot create themselves and must have been created. I do not hesitate to give this mysterious creator the same name that most cultures on earth have given it for thousands of years: God!"

As a young man I began to work in business and climbed the career ladder through various positions in the German business sytem. I reached a point where I began to realize that climbing up was not really going anywhere and I had to admit to myself and especially to my family, that my life was solely dedicated to the company I worked for. I was faced with the questions of awakening: Is this all? Family or career? Are there other ways? Who can help me? How can I help myself?

Looking back, I can understand that at that point I began the path of self-mastery.

Several years of self–discovery followed: I continued in business, but I also learned rebirthing and trained in whitewater kayaking; both were very important on this path. I was often confronted with situations in which I had to overcome fear and was forced to move into completely new and unknown areas of myself. I thank my teachers and friends, Dr. Wolfgang Strasser and Bertold Wichmann, for their special accompaniment. I practiced the rebirthing technique I had been taught for a period of almost five years with an accomplished psychologist. I also thank Angela Rudhardt for the intensive time of our practice.

However, I still felt that I had to keep growing. Then one day I saw a flyer for a workshop which read "Reiki—Heal Yourself! given by Brigitte Müller" It sounded so interesting that I convinced my wife, Edith, to go with me to the workshop. This decision, in the beginning of 1984, opened into a new life for us—but we did not know it yet.

During this 1st Grade workshop, I was surprised to realize that something was changing within me and especially in my hands: I had received the gift of healing hands! I was so inspired by the feeling of this new sensation, that immediately after the workshop my wife and I began to give each other treatments several times a week. The desire to learn more about Reiki grew in us, and we told Brigitte that we wanted to receive the 2nd Reiki Grade, which we did, later that same year. We began to study the specific meaning of the Oku Den, the deeper wisdom of Reiki, while broadening our insights on its general understanding. The most eventful times for us were after each workshop, when we began to integrate what we had learned into our daily lives. We could hardly believe what we were able to do with Reiki. We became so Reiki-ized that we began to enthusiastically organize workshops for Brigitte. During this time, I came to a clear realization: it was phenomenal to experience the positive changes in people during a weekend workshop. It was just wonderful to be allowed to experience this.

One day Brigitte put into words, what I had unconsciously felt or anticipated: she told me that she could imagine me becoming a Reiki master.

I played with this thought in my mind for several months and I talked about it often with my wife. Suddenly I had the clarity within me: I want to become a Reiki Master!

So I wrote to Phyllis Lei Furumoto, the grand master of the Usui System, and applied for the training and initiation to be a Reiki Master. She replied with an invitation to a self-assessment workshop in the United States. I followed this sign, and traveled from Frankfurt to Boise, Idaho.

There were five of us future Reiki Masters participating in the workshop. We encountered each other very openly, and everyone had a chance to share and work on things within themselves. During the course of the workshop, we became mirrors for each other, so that we could see ourselves more clearly. It was left open whether Phyllis would initiate one or several participants of the workshop into Reiki Masters. Then, during the last night—it was already moving towards the morning hours—Phyllis said: "At sunrise I will initiate Horst as a Reiki Master."

It was a perfect surprise, because I had not counted on being initiated—and such a moving experience it was to be initiated as a Reiki Master on that 6th of July, 1985 in the mountains of Bogus Basin, Idaho. Phyllis Lei Furumoto, Michael Hartly, Paul and Susan Mitchell, Brigitte Müller, Hiltrud Marg and I, climbed a beautiful mountain at six-thirty in the morning during sunrise. We had a wonderful panoramic view of the surrounding mountains, forests and the desert. We could all feel the exceptional energies that were released when Phyllis said: "Now is the right time!" I feel such deep gratitude to Phyllis for transferring this energy through the initiation. There are no words to describe it.

I stayed in Boise for the Master training with Phyllis, Susan and Paul Mitchell. Paul gave me the opportunity to assist him in one of his Reiki workshops. Before returning to Germany, I went to visit the Yogananda ashram in Encinitas, California. This gave me a chance to quietly retreat, as a way to reflect on the work of the past weeks. I want to mention the great support I received during this time from my wife, Edith, and our Reiki Master friend Brigitte Müller. And I still think of all the great friends who helped me with their trust and practical support as I began my practice, and continue to do so today.

*

During the entire trip—especially during the long flights and waiting periods—I treated my right elbow with Reiki. Several years back I had been diagnosed with "tennis elbow" and had received medications and injections for it, but the symptoms kept coming back. Although I cannot say exactly how many hours I treated my elbow in the course of the trip, one thing is certain: when I arrived in Germany, I had no pain and could move my arm as if nothing had ever happened to it. To this day, thank God, I have not had any symptoms of tennis elbow.

*

Days, weeks and months passed, filled with the tasks of my work and Reiki. At that time, The *Blue Reiki Book* was translated and printed in German, and Brigitte and I also wrote *The White Reiki Guidebook*, which we distributed to our workshop participants. A lot of Reiki workshops were taking place, and we had the first international Reiki Master conference in Germany, held in Friedrichsdorf, Taunus. It was all a wonderful time, full of rich experiences. But I was still working as a businessman, and deep within me was the urge to stop working and completely give myself to Reiki. I did not see how I could do this, until October 27, 1986.

On that day, early in the morning, something extraordinary happened, which led to a complete change in my life: for inexplicable reasons, I fell sideways in front of a moving car, and for reasons just as inexplicable, I somehow turned myself, or maybe I "was turned" in such a way that I landed lying lengthwise between the two front wheels of the car. The driver was able to stop the car just as my head lay under the car's radiator grill. I suffered many internal and external injuries but I was completely conscious during the entire event, and was intensely aware of the pain and everything going on around me. I felt clearly "Now everything is over." Later I realized the depth of the message: every end brings a new beginning!

So I was forced to rest in order to heal. I was also about to change my life, give up my current occupation and dedicate myself to what I was called for. While I recovered I had to be my own patient, giving myself Reiki—as best I could move—and working with the 2nd Grade Reiki. My loving wife Edith was there every day and gave me Reiki. Dagmar Bock also helped me during the difficult first few days. Phyllis, Brigitte and other Reiki friends came to treat me directly in addition to the many distant Reiki treatments. I will never forget how much my Austrian Reiki friends helped me over that distance on the telephone. It was a wave of willingness to help as I had never experienced before. A spontaneous healing network formed itself and made me feel deeply thankful. I began planning my future while in the hospital and was able to go home in about two weeks.

Although it took me two years, what a joy it was, after exhausting difficulties, to succeed in the practical realization of my independence, *to receive the gift of my own life.*

✳

Here are a few personal experiences which are significant for myself and others:

An acquaintance called me one night and asked me to help J., a 41 year-old mother of two children, who was suffering from advanced cancer. To meet her, I had to drive to a hospital in Rheinland–Pfalz. She had been told that she would never be able to get out of her bed again because her bones would break like glass due to her bone marrow cancer. J. was not only physically but spiritually and mentally in very bad shape. I began working with her on a mental level, and gave her Reiki as I did so. I visited her often, and we had long conversations over the phone. After a certain point I initiated her into the 1st Grade Reiki, so that she could treat herself in my absence. About six weeks later she left the hospital under her own responsibility in an ambulance. Her general condition was much better, and she was able to live with her severe illness.

At home, J. was treated by her family doctor, a sister who took care of her on a daily basis, and a doctor friend who worked with her on a spiritual level from time to time. I visited her often, and it was always an extraordinary gift to be able to treat this woman with Reiki.

One day when we talked on the phone, she said: "You won't have to come to my place next time we meet. I'm driving again and will meet you halfway! I'll take you out to dinner!" I felt overwhelmed with surprise and gratitude, as well as deeply respectful for the universe She really did drive herself to the place we agreed on, and met me there! Tears of joy and thankfulness flowed as we embraced each other. I felt grateful to have been allowed to have such an experience in my life.

J. ultimately moved into her parent's house where she had loving people by her side. This helped her to learn to understand that there *are* universal, divine rules which become reality—though often for us they are incomprehensible. During her last days on this earth, she kept reassuring us that the last two years of her life, had been the most intensive and meaningful time of her life. J. understood, was able to let go, and left us in peace and harmony.

✳

Reiki works on animals, beyond the physical level, as in the case of our dog Anka, a female Dalmatian.

She had been with us for twelve adventure-filled years and had become a real member of the family. But as she got older she began to have physical difficulties, especially in the hip. During our walks, Anka had to stop walking often and would even lie down several times. We would give her Reiki, and she would resume walking at a quick pace without any visible difficulties. But we soon had to realize she was reaching the end of her days. The intervals between treatments became shorter and shorter, and then we had to give her Reiki every day. One day she was doing very badly, and it seemed as if nothing helped anymore. I still remember it clearly: Anka stood in our kitchen and was not able to move at all. I looked at her, put my hands on her head and body… the look she gave me with her eyes was so powerful. There are kinds of vibrations, which are expressed through the physical organs — in this case the dog's eyes—that one can only try to describe. The message I received in her eyes was this: a complete understanding of what was happening, a simultaneous acceptance, which expressed a release, there were no signs of a fight or a cramp in her, although she must have been in a lot of pain. And what was unforgettable for me: her eyes were expressing great thankfulness, like a wave of unconditional love. She died that day. During and after her transformation we accompanied Anka with distant Reiki. It was important for us to send her on her way with light and love.

✳

I want to encourage all Reiki practitioners to be prepared with their healing hands when emergencies occur.

My wife and son and I were in Turkey for a few days and Armin, my son, was enjoying his hobby of skin-diving. One day we watched from the shore as he went out in a small boat with another boy and their diving instructor. Everything seemed to be fine, but all of a sudden we saw a person surface in the water, helping another person in the water. The distance was too far for us to see who it was, but we could see clearly that one of the divers was receiving first-aid out there in the water! *We immediately began sending distant Reiki!* Now one of the divers was pulled into the small boat and my wife and I were obviously very worried, since one of them was our son. As the boat came closer to the shore, we could see that the diving instructor was the person steering the boat and our son had put his hands on the chest of the other diver, who appeared motionless. Suddenly there were several women next to us, and one began to weep loudly—she was the boy's mother. Everyone helped to get the boat and its passengers onto the shore. Without hesitating, I asked the boy's mother if I could treat him until a doctor arrived. She asked how, and I told her I would apply my hands. She looked at me skeptically, but after considering the situation, agreed. I began using the emergency Reiki positions and started to communicate with the boy's higher self. After about fifteen minutes he opened his eyes and looked helplessly and weakly at the crowd around him. It was not until then that he realized that he was being treated. His mother was beside herself with joy and thanked me, but the boy did not want to be touched any more. I recommended that they consult a doctor immediately. After the excitement had settled, our son told us that the boy, who was about his age, had begun to panic under water and resurfaced much too fast without his mask. During that moment of shock and fear, my son Armin had already begun an emergency Reiki treatment in the water.

✳

Another time I was in the South of France with my family. One of the attractions offered on the beach was parasailing. We went to look because I had always wanted to try it, and I ended up doing a wonderful flight. After I had landed, a young woman began to prepare for her flight, while I watched. While trying to get off the ground, running fast, she was unable to steer her parachute quite right and was hit from the side by some wind, ending up being uncontrollably dragged over the beach and the shore. The parachute ripped a wooden fence out of the ground and hit another woman in the head. She cried out loudly and fell to the ground, blood running down her head. Everyone stared helplessly at the injured woman. An inner flash went through me and I ran to the scene, yelling for someone to call a doctor, and began the emergency treatment, which also works for shock and fear. Despite her open head wound, the woman stopped screaming and was able to consciously look at me, and through her eyes I saw that she felt taken care of, had trust in me and was quiet. This took about ten minutes, then the paramedics arrived.

✳

I had an especially deep experience with my friend's father during his last hours. He was in the hospital, fighting for his life on earth. He did not want to let go. He expressed this by sitting up in his bed, rocking up and down, and trying to literally hold on to what could not be held anymore. That was how I found him. Everything had been done for him, he was medically and technically well taken care of. In the presence of his family, I put my hands on him in different and specific places. Already after three or four minutes, his tightness and his cramps let go. He stopped rocking back and forth in his bed, which surprised everyone, since I hadn't said a word to him. I had constant eye contact with him and was able to read the sudden change in his eyes. He was unable to speak, but in his eyes I could read, "I have understood, everything is all right, I am now able to let go." And he did. It was a completely new experience for me, and took me some time to integrate it. I came to understand it as a gift.

✳

On this path, I am surprised at the way Reiki affects things connected with my everyday life—often in relation to objects or technical machinery. I want to share one of many instances.

On a break during the Reiki Master conference on the big island, Hawaii, a lady from our camp, who was a fellow Reiki Master from Greece, and I, drove to the next larger town. Along the way we had to get gas. There were two keys, one for the ignition and one for the gas-cap. When the gas station attendant returned the keys to the driver, they got mixed up, and suddenly the gas cap key was stuck in the ignition! Nothing would move it. It wouldn't come out or turn either way. All four of us gave it a try: the driver, the attendant, the Greek lady and I, all with our own little tricks and ways, but nothing happened. Sitting in the back seat, I sent Reiki onto the key, but there was no movement. Having tried all this, the gas attendant called someone else, who came over with a huge monkey wrench like I had never seen before. Our driver took one look at it and said please! stop! it was not even her car, she had only borrowed it from someone else in the camp. I asked to give Reiki one more try before this guy with his huge wrench could do possible damage. I traded seats with the driver, and began to give the ignition Reiki. After about three or four minutes, I felt that it was done. I took my hands away, touched the key with my thumb and index finger, pulled up lightly, and without any force the key came loose. I was very grateful for Reiki. Besides my Greek colleague and I, nobody around understood what had just happened. The attendant with the huge wrench actually looked quite disappointed, as if we had gotten in the way of his special service.

✳

In the course of the conference, we also visited Mrs. Hawayo Takata's last resting place in Hilo in Hawaii. The following photo shows the church where Mrs. Takata's urn is kept:

Mrs. Hawayo's resting place.

On our way home from the church to where we were staying in Kalani Honua, we received an extra special goodbye gift from the heavens—a beam of light from above—which I was able to capture in this photo:

In 1987 my Reiki path also brought me to the important Reiki cities of Japan: Kyoto and Tokyo, as well as Japan's holy mountain, Fujiyama. My family and I had many uplifting moments while traveling through this beautiful country. Reiki was our constant companion. We kept thinking that it was here that Dr. Usui rediscovered and unfolded Reiki. In Nara, the old city of the emperor, close to Kyoto, I took the following picture of Japan's largest temple, the Nara Daibutsu:

The temple Nara Daibutsu.

I also believe that Reiki has allowed my creative abilities to unfold. Because of the integration of its power in my daily life, I have been able to recognize the needs of the people around me, and have discovered ways to meet them. Out of this came a method of life supporting treatments which my wife and I have been teaching in workshops since 1989, which we call CREAMO. This wonderful power helps in its own way to find and develop a person's talent.

With these personal experiences, I want to encourage all people, no matter what kinds of careers or occupations they are involved in to learn and use Reiki; to give our family, neighbors, friends, animals and plants. This is what our planet needs so desperately, a special kind of healing: Love.

When I look at the past today, I realize how Reiki has completely changed my life. Being a Reiki master, I am aware that I can still contribute to the circulation of Reiki, so that its loving energy will find access to all people. My personal development reached a completely new dimension with Phyllis Lei

Furumoto's permission allowing me to train and initiate other Reiki Masters. It is a humble feeling of gratitude to carry Reiki on in this way. Besides the U.S. and Europe it is being taught in India, Brazil, Africa, Hungary and Russia—all over the world.

My wife Edith and I are very grateful to transmit light and love to all living things with Reiki.

Horst H. Günther

AFTERWORD

We, Brigitte and Horst, hope that you enjoyed this book on Reiki. We would like to thank you for taking the time to give yourself an inside view of Reiki.

We hope that if you now feel the desire to receive the "gift of healing hands," that your path will lead you to *your* Reiki Master.

If you have already been initiated into Reiki, then we are glad to have you connected with you, and hope that this book may have given you further inspiration.

May love, peace and joy be with you!

Important Note

Again and again we get letters or calls from people who went to a Reiki seminar and who did not experience any change of energy in their hands, or did not benefit from any healing process, but the opposite. These people sometimes complained that they feel worse and that they did not experience anything that our book describes.

After some of these people finally had the chance to be initiated by us into the first and second degree, they affirmed the presence of Reiki in them, and that the healing process occurred.

That is why we want to raise the awareness of what to look for when you choose a Reiki Master:

In the last years, a lot of people participated in Reiki crash courses, or just one or two weekends of training, without following the traditional way of learning Reiki. The practice of Reiki has been diluted and abused.

People who became Reiki Masters that way, in general, did not develop their capacity to transfer or teach Reiki. In the tradition of Dr. Usui,

Reiki has been handed down as an oral teaching. That means that a competent energy transfer can only take place through a direct contact with a living Reiki Master who has been initiated in that lineage.

Grandmaster Hawayo Takata once said, "Those who abuse Reiki, will lose it." We see the truth of this in the messages we get from the people.

For your own good, learn to differentiate. It is important that you follow the line of initiated Masters. It would be good to know how long a Master has practiced the first, second, and the Master degree, and by whom he has been initiated.

In general, a person who wants to become a Master should have three years of experience in practicing the first and second degree, and should have an apprenticeship with a Master for about one year before being initiated into a Master himself. It needs the individualized teaching and supervision over a longer period of time, not only for the learning, but also to allow your own process of soul and mind integration. The now initiated Master should have about six years (up to now three years) experience as a Master, and Reiki seminar leader before he conducts the great responsibility to guide other students to Mastership.

All this information will support you in your decision to choose when you are looking for an experienced Reiki practitioner or Master.

We wish that you receive the gift of Reiki healing hands.

Brigitte Müller and Horst H. Günther

APPENDIX

ADDITIONAL INFORMATION:

Inquiries about Reiki workshops with the authors of this book may be sent to the following address:

> Brigitte Müller & Horst H. Günther
> Postfach 15
> D-61381 Friedrichsdorf
> Germany

An address list of international Reiki Masters is available through The Reiki Alliance:

> The Reiki Alliance
> P.O. Box 41
> Cataldo, ID 83810
> USA

Information about the VERANA © color–foils is available through:
> Vera Suchanek
> Lohmühle 1
> D-79206 Breisach
> Germany

Bibliography

• Bach, Edward
  The Bach Flower Remedies. Keats, 1979.
  Heal Thyself. Sun Pubs., 1985.
  The Twelve Healers & Other Remedies. Sun Pubs., 1988.
• Baginski, Bodo & Shalila Sharamon
  Reiki, Universal Life Energy. LifeRhythm, 1988.
  The Chakra Handbook, Blue Dolphine,
• Blum, Ralph
  The Book of Runes. Oracle Books, 1982.
• Brown, Fran
  Living Reiki: Takata's Teachings. LifeRhythm, 1992.
• Burka, Christa F.
  Clearing Crystal Consciousness. Bro Life Inc., 1986.
  Pearls of Consciousness. Bro Life Inc., 1987.
• Cerminara, Gina
  Insights for the Age of Aquarius. Theos. Pub House, 1976.
  Many Lives, Many Loves. DeVorss, 1981.
  Many Mansions: The Edgar Cayce Story on Reincarnation. NAL-Dutton, 1988.
• Diamond, John
  Life Energy. Paragon House, 1990.
  Your Body Doesn't Lie. Warner Books, 1989.
• Gawain, Shakti
  Living in the Light. New World Library, 1986.
• Haberly, Helen
  Reiki. Hawayo Takata's Story. Archidigm Publications, 1990.
• Hay, Louise
  Heal Your Body. Hay House, 1988.
  You Can Heal Your Life. Hay House, 1987.
• Jampolsky, Gerald G.
  Goodbye to Guilt. Bantam, 1985.
  Love is Letting Go of Fear. Celestial Arts, 1988.
  One Person Can Make a Difference. Bantam, 1992.

Love Is the Answer. Bantam, 1991.
Out of Darkness Into the Light., Bantam 1989.
* Kelder, Peter
  The Eye of Revelation: The Original Five Tibetan Rites of Rejuvenation. Borderland Sciences, 1989.
* Kubler-Ross, Elizabeth
  Living with Death & Dying. Macmillan, 1982.
  On Death & Dying. Macmillan, 1970.
  On Life After Death. Celestial Arts, 1991.
* Moody, Raymond
  The Light Beyond. Bantam, 1989.
* Nelson, Ruby
  Door of Everything. DeVorss, 1963.
* Price, John R.
  The Abundance Book. Quartus Books, 1987.
  The Planetary Commission. Quartus Books, 1984.
  Practical Spirituality. Quartus Books, 1985.
* Purce, Jill
  The Mystic Spiral. Thames Hudson, 1980.
* Ray, Sondra
  Pure Joy. Celestial Arts, 1988.
  The Only Diet There Is. Celestial Arts, 1981.
  Loving Relationships. Celestial Arts, 1980.
* Sams, Jamie and David Carson
  Medicine Cards. Bear & Co., 1988.
* Scheffer, Mechthild
  Bach Flower Therapy. Inner Traditions, 1987.
* Smothermon, Ron
  Winning Through Enlightenment. 1980.
* Yogananda, Paramahansa
  Autobiography of a Yogi. Self Realization Fellowship, 1981.
  Scientific Healing Affirmations. 1981

The Original Voice
LIVING REIKI: TAKATA'S TEACHINGS

Stories from the Life of Hawayo Takata
as told to
Fran Brown

In this loving memoir to her teacher, Fran Brown has gathered the colorful stories told by Hawayo Takata during her thirty-five years as the only Reiki Master teaching. The stories create an inspirational panorama of Takata's teachings, filled with the practical and spiritual aspects of a life given to healing.

Reiki is the energy of life. In the Usui System of Natural Healing, this energy is honored and used as a guide in daily life. It offers a simple path to perceive and experience our lives as a sacred honorable experience. These stories are illustrations from the life of a woman who lived the Reiki teachings. They are funny and serious, happy and sad, representing her own Japanese/Hawaiian upbringing and always demonstrating her deep trust in the Life Energy. The stories also show the growth of Takata's healing power and the simplicity with which she accepted it. From humble beginnings she became a great figure of strength, loved and respected by all who knew her.

The Original Book
REIKI, UNIVERSAL LIFE ENERGY

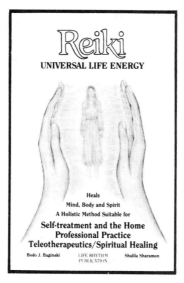

by Bodo Baginski & Shalila Sharamon
200 pages, illustrations

This original book on Reiki is read in many languages around the world, spreading its pure message to all who search for light and healing.

While the roots of Reiki reach far back into the ancient origins of natural healing, the method presented here has been rediscovered in modern times and is now well on the way to becoming a widely practiced form of folk medicine. More and more practitioners, therapists and healers are making reiki part of their therapeutic program, or are practicing this method exclusively; but above all, Reiki is being used by more and more nonprofessionals as a most effective means of promoting health and well-being.

This book features a unique compilation and interpretation of over 200 psychosomatic symptoms and diseases.

LifeRhythm Publications

John C. Pierrakos M.D CORE ENERGETICS
Developing the Capacity to Love and Heal
With 16 pages of four-color illustrations of human auras corresponding to their character structure,
300 pages
John C. Pierrakos, M.D., is a psychiatrist, body-therapist and an authority on consciousness and human energy fields. The focus of his work is to open the "Core" of his patients to a new awareness of how body, emotions, mind , will and spirituality form a unit. Dr. Pierrakos is considered one of the founders of a whole new movement in therapeutic work, integrating body, mind and spirit and this book has become classic.

Fran Brown LIVING REIKI: TAKATA'S TEACHINGS
Stories from the Life of Hawayo Takata
110 pages
In this loving memoir to her teacher, Fran Brown has gathered the colorful stories told by Hawayo Takata during her thirty-five years s the only Reiki Master Teaching. The stories create an inspirational panorama of Takata's teachings, filled with the practical and spiritual aspects of a life given to healing.

Malcolm Brown, Ph.D. THE HEALING TOUCH
An Introduction to Organismic Psychotherapy
320 pages 38 illustrations
A moving and meticulous account of Malcolm Brown's journey from Rogerian-style verbal psychotherapist to gifted body psychotherapist. Dr. Brown developed his own art and science of body psychotherapy with the purpose of re-activating the natural mental/spiritual polarities of the embodied soul and transcendental psyche. Using powerful case histories as examples, Brown describes in theory and practice the development of his work; the techniques to awaken the energy flow and its integration with the main Being centers: Eros, Logos, the Spritual Warrior and the Hara.

Bodo Baginski & Shalila Sharamon REIKI Universal Life Energy
200 pages illustrations
Reiki is described as the energy which forms the basis of all life. With the help of specific methods, anyone can learn to awaken and activate this universal life energy so that healing and harmonizing energy flows through the hands. Reiki is healing energy in the truest sense of the word, leading to greater individual harmony and attunement to the basic forces of the universe. This book features a unique compilation and interpretation, from the author's experience, of over 200 psychosomatic symptoms and diseases

Allan Sachs D.C. GRAPEFRUIT SEED EXTRACT
A Natural Alternative to Antibiotics
100 pages
Dr. Allan Sachs' innovative work in treating sufferers from Candida Albicans imbalance, fool allergies and environmental illness has inspired thousands of patients and a generation of like-minded physicians. Based on his training as a medical researcher at New York's Downstate Medical Center and his life-long interest in plants, he undertook an intense study of the antimicrobial aspects of certain plant derivatives. This complete handbook gives all information on the theraputic use of grapefruit seeds and also details their use for many household, farming and industrial needs.

Ron Kurtz **BODY-CENTERED PSYCHOTHERAPY: THE HAKOMI METHOD**

The Integrated Use of Mindfulness, Nonviolence and the Body

212 pages, illustrations

Hakomi is a synthesis of philosphies, techniques and approaches that has its own unique artistry, form and organic process. Some of its origins stem from Eastern philosphic concepts of gentleness, compassion, mindfulness and going with grain— as well as general systems theory, which incorporates the idea of respect for the wisdom of each individual as a living organic system that spontaneously organizes matter and energy and selects from the environment what it needs to maintain its goals, programs and identity.

Helmut G. Sieczka **CHAKRA BREATHING**

A Pathway to Energy and Harmony

100 pages Illustrations   Supplemental Cassette Tape of Guided Meditations

A guide to self-healing, this book is meant to help activate and harmonize the energy centers of the subtle body. The breath is the bridge between body and soul. In today's world as our lives are determined by stressful careers and peak performance, the silent and meditative moments have become more vital. Remembering our true selves, our natural energy balances are restored. Chakra-breathing enhances this kind of awareness and transformational work, especially on the emotional and energetic level.

R. Stamboliev **THE ENERGETICS OF VOICE DIALOGUE**

Exploring the Energetics of Transformational Psychology

100 pages

Voice Dialogue is a therapeutic technique based on the transformational model of consciousness. This book approaches the human psyche as a synthesis of experience-patterns which may be modified only when the original pattern of an experience has been touched, understood and felt from an adult, integrated perspective, developing an "Aware Ego". This book explores the energetic aspects of the relationship between client and therapist, offering exercises for developing energetic skills and giving case histories to illustrate these skills. Voice Dialogue is the work of Hal and Sidra Stone Ph.Ds.

R. Flatischler **THE FORGOTTEN POWER OF RHYTHM**

TA KE TI NA

160 pages, illustrations   Supplemental CD or Cassette

Rhythm is the central power of our lives; it connects us all. There is a powerful source of rhythmic knowledge in every human being. Reinhard Flatischler presents his brilliant approach to rhythm is this book, for both the layman and the professional musician. TA KE TI NA offers an experience of the interaction of pulse, breath, voice, walking and clapping which awakens our inherent rhythm in the most direct way— through the body. It provides a new understanding of the many musical voices of our world.

John C. Pierrakos M.D. **EROS, LOVE & SEXUALITY**

The Unifying Forces of Life and Relationship

150 pages

The free flow of the three great forces of life—eros, love and sexuality—is our greatest source of pleasure. These three forces are simply different aspects of the life force, and when we stay open, they are experienced as one. They generate all activity, all creativity. This book has been long awaited. John Pierrakos, the great psychiatrist, was a student and colleague of Wilhelm Reich, and co-founder of Bioenergetics; he later developed his own therapeutic work, Core Energetics, which integrates the higher dimensions into our physical existence.

LIFERHYTHM

PO Box 806   Mendocino CA 95460   USA
Phone: (707) 937-1825   Fax: (707) 937-3052
e-mail: books@liferhythm.com   http://www.liferhythm.com